READING TONI MORRISON

Recent Titles in
The Pop Lit Book Club

READING
TONI MORRISON

Rachel Lister

The Pop Lit Book Club

GREENWOOD PRESS
An Imprint of ABC-CLIO, LLC

A B C 🔹 C L I O

Santa Barbara, California • Denver, Colorado • Oxford, England

Library of Congress Cataloging-in-Publication Data

Lister, Rachel.
   Reading Toni Morrison / Rachel Lister.
     p. cm. — (The pop lit book club)
   Includes bibliographical references and index.
     ISBN 978-0-313-35499-1 (acid-free paper)—ISBN 978-0-313-35500-4 (ebook)
1. Morrison, Toni—Criticism and interpretation. I. Title.
   PS3563.O8749Z755   2009
   813'.54—dc22   2009020273

13 12 11 10 09 1 2 3 4 5

This book is also available on the World Wide Web as an eBook.
Visit www.abc-clio.com for details.

ABC-CLIO, LLC
130 Cremona Drive, P. O. Box 1911
Santa Barbara, California 93116–1911

This book is printed on acid-free paper. ∞

Manufactured in the United States of America

CONTENTS

PREFACE

Reading Toni Morrison is an informative and accessible guide to Toni Morrison's novels, ranging from *The Bluest Eye* (1970) to *Love* (2003). The guide offers analysis of Morrison's formal and narrative poetics and explores her engagement with contemporary issues and popular culture. It aims to introduce Morrison's work to new readers and to open up lines of inquiry to those already familiar with her novels. Discussion questions are provided both to focus and develop readings.

The opening chapter of the guide gives an outline of Morrison's life and career. Drawing from a range of interviews and her novels, this chapter provides insight into the ways in which Morrison's heritage and personal experiences have informed her work. It also examines Morrison's revelations concerning the conception of her novels, her writing methodology, and her thoughts on the role of the contemporary writer.

"Toni Morrison and the Novel" examines Morrison's vision of the novel form and her engagement with the aesthetics and narrative conventions of black oral and musical traditions. This chapter considers the relationship between Morrison's formal strategies and thematic concerns. It addresses the issue of genre, looking at the various ways in which critics have categorized her fiction and examining her response to these classifications. Individual readings of Morrison's novels follow this chapter. They place the novels in context and provide analysis of thematic concerns, characterization, language, and imagery. Particular emphasis is placed on Morrison's handling of themes that extend across her fiction: the different forms and manifestations of love, the pull of the past, and the relationship between self and community.

"Today's Issues in Toni Morrison's Work" examines the contemporary relevance of Morrison's fiction. The chapter draws from Morrison's commentary on race, class, and gender in today's America and goes on to analyze her handling of these issues in her fiction. It addresses Morrison's concerns about the impact of consumerist ideology and its attendant notions of success and analyzes her elaboration of alternative narratives and models for the contemporary reader.

The chapter "Pop Culture in Toni Morrison's Work" explores Morrison's engagement with popular culture. It delivers analysis of her representation of popular culture and its various discourses in her fictional world and ends with a discussion of Jonathan Demme's film *Beloved*, to date the only cinematic adaptation of Morrison's work. This section also considers the reception of the film and Morrison's thoughts on the adaptation process. "Toni Morrison on the Internet" offers guidance to the wealth of online resources available to Morrison's readers. It provides an overview of online interviews, articles, and reviews, as well as some critical material on Morrison's novels.

Morrison's relationship with the media is the focus of "Toni Morrison and the Media." It explores how Morrison has used the media to reach a wider audience and to engage in public debates. Morrison's scrutiny of the media's language is also addressed here; the chapter considers her analysis of the media's role in manipulating public opinion and perpetuating racial and social stereotypes. This chapter also examines Morrison's response to the critical reception of her work.

The final chapter is a guide to readers seeking fiction that shares thematic concerns with Morrison's oeuvre or that encourages a similar level of reader involvement. This chapter draws on Morrison's commentaries on books that she has enjoyed or that have influenced her in some way, and considers works by writers who have identified Morrison as an influence or expressed an interest in her concerns.

I thank my editors at Greenwood, Kaitlin Ciarmiello and George Butler, for their considerable patience, guidance, and encouragement. My appreciation also goes to Anne Talvacchio for her patience and hard work during the production of this book. Many thanks also go to Pamela Knights for her years of support and Diana Collecott for introducing me to Toni Morrison. As always I am deeply grateful to Mum, Dad, and Brian for their unfailing support.

1

TONI MORRISON: A WRITER'S LIFE

In January 1998, shortly after the publication of her seventh novel *Paradise*, Toni Morrison gave a television interview to journalist Charlie Rose. After asking her about her latest novel, Rose turned to the subject of Morrison's life. Her response was to enact dozing off. In 2003, after the publication of her next novel, *Love*, Rose raised the subject again, suggesting that Morrison write her life story. She expressed surprise at such a notion, telling Rose that her daily life is not appropriate material for an autobiography; it is her "imagination" that is compelling.[1] From Morrison's perspective, the writer should be measured by her "ability ... to imagine what is *not* the self, to familiarize the strange and mystify the familiar."[2] As early as 1976, Morrison noted a movement away from autobiographical renderings in her fiction. Speaking to Robert Stepto, she observed that the representation of community in her third novel, *Song of Solomon*, differs from that of her first, *The Bluest Eye*, where she was drawing on autobiographical material.[3]

Morrison was born Chloe Ardelia Wofford in 1931. She became known as Toni during her undergraduate years at Howard University. She has explained that she felt much vexation upon seeing the name "Toni Morrison" rather than her real name on the cover of her first novel, *The Bluest Eye*. She originally submitted the manuscript under the name Toni Morrison because it was familiar to her editor.[4]

Morrison was born and raised in Lorain, Ohio, a town populated by immigrants mainly from Europe. At her integrated school she met

> Many accounts of Morrison's life give her name as Chloe Anthony
> Wofford. However, John Duvall reports that the middle name
> "Ardelia" appears on Morrison's birth certificate (Duvall, 330).

children from a range of cultural backgrounds, some of whom she taught to read. She recalls that Lorain offered little in the way of spectacular scenery or architecture but has speculated that this might have proved "conducive to a fecund imagination."[5] It is the language of the African American community of Lorain that she remembers most vividly and that would come to infuse her fiction: a powerful discourse emerged from the combination of "new language and biblical language and sermonic language and standard language" heard in her hometown.[6]

Morrison, the second of four children, speaks of her childhood as an enriching and stimulating time. When she is asked to speak about her early years, salient images and feelings resurface persistently; the sounds of her childhood had particular resonance. She recalls listening to music—both of Morrison's maternal grandparents were musicians— being uplifted by the sound of her mother's singing, and following the exchange of stories between family members and friends.

Memories of her father's ghost stories are particularly vivid. Morrison's mother Ella Ramah Willis Wofford was a homemaker and her father George Wofford was a ship welder. Both had come to Ohio from the South searching for a better life and hoping to find a space beyond the gaze of a racist white society. From her parents Morrison learned lessons that have guided her throughout her life. Her response to racism was informed by her father, who reminded her that she did not inhabit the "imagination" of racist people. She has "always looked upon the acts of racist exclusion or insult, as pitiable, from the other person" and "always thought that there was something deficient—intellectually, emotionally—about such people."[7]

When asked to identify sources of inspiration for her imaginative world, Morrison points to the stories and experiences of her ancestors. Personal experience rarely finds a direct route into her novels but has ignited prolonged consideration of particular concepts or focalizations. Speaking to Anne Koenen about the conception of "self-invented" women in her fiction, such as *Sula*'s Eva and *Song of Solomon*'s Pilate, Morrison is reminded of an experience from her youth.[8] She recalls being in a room with her mother, grandmother, and great-grandmother and recognizing her own place as a descendant of this line of women.

The impact of this formidable apprehension resonated powerfully with Morrison; readers see its influence in the representation of Pilate's woman-centered family in *Song of Solomon*.[9] Morrison called on her recently deceased father for other narratives and discourses in *Song of Solomon*, the first of her novels to place masculine experience at its center. In the foreword to the Vintage edition of the novel, she reveals that the narrative took shape only after she asked her father's ghost to describe the men he knew; his responses laid the foundations for the main narrative line.

A further episode that has greatly informed Morrison's fiction is recorded in her introduction to Robert Bergman's collection of photographs, *A Kind of Rapture*, in which she details a revealing encounter with an old fisherwoman. The woman told Morrison that she fished most days in the water on a neighbor's property. Sensing a strong connection with this woman, Morrison sought her out again but she never reappeared; the neighbor, whose permission the fisherwoman claimed she had been given, knew nothing of her. Speculating on her powerful desire to engage further with the fisherwoman, Morrison realizes that she was "missing some aspect of [her]self, and that there are no strangers."[10] This epiphany sheds light on some of the more mysterious encounters in Morrison's fiction. In *Paradise*, Consolata and Dovey register a powerful sense of connection with apparently strange men who seem to reflect facets of themselves back to them.

Morrison's first encounters with literature came at an early age. Indeed, she has often stated that she cannot recall her pre-literate life. It would be some years, however, before she would encounter African American literature; it was not taught in the integrated school that she attended. During her teenage years, Morrison cleaned houses after school; she told Claudia Dreifus that she found some interest in using housekeeping "gadgets" that she had not used before. While some of the people she worked for were "nice," others were "terrible." She drew on this experience in *The Bluest Eye* in her portrayal of Pauline Breedlove, a mother who, forced to raise her children in squalor, is ignored by society unless she speaks or acts in her role as a maid for a white household.[11] Morrison graduated from high school in 1949 and moved to Washington, D.C., to attend Howard University. Here she met her future husband, architect Harold Morrison, and joined the Howard University Players. On her travels with the theater group, she visited the South for the first time. This experience, along with memories of her parents' accounts, would greatly inform her fictional representations of the South. After graduating from Howard in 1953, she went on to study English at postgraduate level at Cornell University. She earned her master's degree in 1955, writing her thesis on "The Treatment of the Alienated Subject" in the literature of modernist writers William Faulkner and Virginia Woolf. Morrison taught English at Texas Southern University before returning to Howard to teach. In 1958, she married Harold Morrison. They had two sons, Harold Ford and Slade Kevin, and divorced after six years.

From 1965 until 1983, Morrison worked for the publishing company Random House in New York, eventually becoming a senior editor. There she made it her main priority to find and publish writers whose narratives had yet to be heard or read. Morrison is now recognized for playing a significant role in revitalizing the market for black literature in the 1970s, both as a novelist and a publisher. In *Loose Canons*, a study of multiculturalism in the United States, Henry Louis Gates Jr. notes that there was some resistance among publishers to the work of African American writers during the 1970s. He credits this to growing unease with some of the political campaigns of the time and notes that Morrison countered this resistance, continuing to publish literature by black writers from all over the world.[12]

It was while working at Random House and raising her two children in Syracuse, New York, that Morrison began to write her first novel. While teaching at Howard University she had joined a writing group, for which she had produced a short story about a black girl who longed for blue eyes; this short narrative, which was favorably received by other members of the group, would provide the foundation for *The Bluest Eye*. From the beginning Morrison regarded the act of writing as "a very long, sustained reading process—except that [she] was the one producing the words."[13] She worked on the novel while her children were asleep and found that in writing this story, she could gain entry into "an unsullied place of envisioning and imagining."[14] Indeed, since writing *The Bluest Eye*, Morrison has experienced very few periods when she has not felt the exhilarating pull of an idea for a new narrative. After being rejected many times, *The Bluest Eye* was published by Holt, Rinehart and Winston in 1970. To date, the rest of Morrison's novels have been published by Alfred A. Knopf. In the afterword to *The Bluest Eye*, Morrison recalls the tenor of the novel's first reviews: "With very few exceptions, the initial publication of *The Bluest Eye* was like Pecola's life: dismissed, trivialized, misread."[15] By 1974, *The Bluest Eye* was no longer in print. Morrison's second novel, *Sula* (1973), was subject to further misreading but generally fared better with the critics. The novel earned Morrison further recognition with a nomination for the National Book Award in 1975. *Sula* was an alternate Book-of-the-Month Club selection and won the Ohioana Book Award. Most significantly, it was through writing this novel that Morrison felt that she had found her individual writing style: "That book seemed to suggest that I had hit on a voice that was mine, that I didn't write like anybody else."[16]

Critics and readers of Morrison's work remain fascinated by this early period of her career. In interviews she is often asked to explain how she found the time to write while raising two children alone. In response she refers to a crucial moment when she sensed the need to evaluate her life and reached the realization that she must respond to two callings: she must be a mother to her children and write. We hear echoes of this strategy in *Song of Solomon* when Pilate asks herself what she must do first to survive and then to live an authentic, meaningful life. With the publication of *Song of Solomon* in 1977, Morrison extended her readership widely. The novel was very well received and went on to win several prestigious literary prizes, including the National Book Critics Circle Award and the American Academy and Institute of Arts and Letters Award. *Song of Solomon* was a Book-of-the-Month Club selection, the first by an African American writer since Richard Wright's *Native Son* in 1940. The novel's publication is now regarded as a milestone in African American culture, so much so that Henry Louis Gates Jr. refers to "the post-*Song of Solomon* ... era of black writing."[17] Morrison has identified the publication of the novel and its subsequent success as a pivotal time not only in her career but in her personal trajectory: only after this novel's release did she claim the identity of writer. She had previously referred to herself first and foremost as a publisher who happened to write novels; she has since recognized this hesitation to claim the identity of writer as a particularly female trait.

Morrison's first three novels were published in the 1970s, the beginning of a particularly rich period for black women's writing. As well as Morrison's three novels, the decade brought the publication of Alice Walker's first novel (*The Third Life of Grange Copeland*), short-story collections by Toni Cade Bambara (*Gorilla My Love* and *The Sea Birds Are Still Alive*), and *I Know Why the Caged Bird Sings*, the first in Maya Angelou's best-selling series of autobiographies. Commentators on African American literature have singled out Morrison as the first woman novelist to give such full expression to the experience of black girls and women. She has often contested this, pointing to novels by Zora Neale Hurston and Paule Marshall. When Morrison is asked to comment on the status of contemporary black women's writing, she stresses its diversity. In an interview for *The World: The Journal of the Unitarian Universalist Association*, she was asked if there are advantages to teaching the works of black women together; she replied that it "can't hurt" but added that she is happy to be taught alongside writers from a range of time periods and cultural matrices: "I don't mind being taught with Alice Walker, William Shakespeare, Milton, Marguerite Duras, or anybody."[18] Several times throughout her career she has noted that the publishing world and the media seem to have room for only one commercially successful black woman writer at a time. She has often expressed her frustration at the disappointing sales of work by black women that she has published such as the novels of Gayl Jones and the poetry of June Jordan.

In 1980, Morrison was elected to the National Council on the Arts. Her fourth novel, *Tar Baby*, appeared one year later. To date, it is the only novel in Morrison's canon that takes place primarily outside of the United States. Its setting is a fictional Caribbean island called Isle des Chevaliers, where a white millionaire named Valerian has attempted to construct his own version of paradise. Morrison has explained that she wanted to put her characters in a "pressure cooker" which forced them to confront those issues that they have suppressed or denied.[19] On the island, the characters are compelled to deal with the buried tensions which surface on the arrival of Son, a black man who challenges their conceptions of themselves and their identity politics. In 1981, Morrison was elected to the American Academy of Arts and Letters and appeared on the front cover of the March 30 edition of *Newsweek*. When told she was to achieve this "coup of the cover," she responded: "The day you put a middle-aged, gray-haired colored lady on the [cover of the] magazine, I will know the revolution is over."[20] She was the first black woman to feature on the cover of the magazine since writer and anthropologist Zora Neale Hurston in 1943.

Another significant turning point for Morrison occurred in 1983. She left her job as editor at Random House after people had voiced concerns that her work as a writer might compromise her editorial duties. Morrison has often spoken of this time as one of exhilarating freedom as she engaged with narratives that were waiting to be told. While collecting material for *The Black Book* (1974), a compilation of visual and textual documents chronicling African American history, Morrison had encountered various stories that would form the foundation for a thematically linked trilogy of novels. At the center of each narrative was a different incarnation of love: one took the form of a newspaper report on a woman named Margaret Garner who had killed her child and tried to kill herself and her other children in order to prevent their return to slavery; another narrative emerged from various newspaper clippings reporting the migration of blacks to Oklahoma, having been told by towns of ex-slaves to "Come Prepared or Not at All"; and a third narrative was captured in a photograph by James Van der Zee of a dying young woman who had been shot by her boyfriend but refused to reveal the name of her killer.

The encounter with Margaret Garner's story inspired the conception of Morrison's fifth novel, *Beloved* (1987). In the foreword to the Vintage edition of the novel, Morrison writes of her realization of the magnitude of her task: to enter and to invite readers into "the repellant landscape" of slavery "was to pitch a tent in a cemetery inhabited by highly vocal ghosts."[21] Morrison found the historical figure of Margaret Garner deeply compelling but she sought a further source of inspiration for her fictional representation. As she sat in front of her home on the Hudson River, a young woman emerged from the water. Here was the "figure most central to the story ... the murdered, not the murderer, the one who lost everything and had no say in any of it."[22] A conversation with writer Gloria Naylor in 1985 reveals that Morrison initially intended to explore the stories of Margaret Garner and the dying woman in Van der Zee's photograph within the boundaries of one novel.[23] However, upon receiving the first part of the manuscript, the publisher decided that it should stand alone as an autonomous work. *Beloved* would become Morrison's most famous, celebrated, and studied novel. On its publication, it received almost universal praise and was awarded the Pulitzer Prize, the Robert F. Kennedy Award, and the Frederic G. Melcher Book Award. In 2006, the *New York Times Book Review* named *Beloved* the best American novel of the past twenty-five years. Morrison herself does not consider *Beloved* to be her best work, but has explained why she believes that it has maintained this reputation. She told Charlie Rose in 2003 that readers feel the significance of engaging with its subject matter: the novel is about "'it,' slavery," a subject that "is so big and full of sensation."[24]

Works of social and literary criticism followed *Beloved*. In 1992, Morrison edited and introduced a collection of essays on the Clarence Thomas hearings, entitled *Race-ing Justice, En-gendering Power: Essays on Anita Hill, Clarence Thomas, and the Construction of Social Reality*. Her seminal work of literary criticism, *Playing in the Dark: Whiteness and the Literary Imagination* (1992), explores how "the Africanist presence informs in compelling and inescapable ways the texture of American literature." Through her readings she reveals how the concerns of canonized works of fiction are "activated by a complex of awareness and employment of a constituted Africanism."[25] *Playing in the Dark* opens up new avenues of inquiry into much-analyzed works of literature such as Mark Twain's *The Adventures of Huckleberry Finn*, Herman Melville's *Moby Dick*, and the short stories of Edgar Allan Poe. Reviews of *Playing in the Dark* were quick to acknowledge its originality and to predict, correctly, its significant influence on the practice of literary criticism. Morrison has revealed that she experienced some animosity from academics who questioned her credentials for this kind of writing. Again, she encountered resistance to the possibility of transcending the boundaries of professional fields.

In 1992, the second novel in Morrison's "love" trilogy was published. Set in Harlem in the 1920s, *Jazz* explores the lives of married couple Joe and Violet Trace, who joined the Great Migration to the city from Virginia. Interwoven with their experiences of urban life are the buried stories of their ancestors from the antebellum South. Morrison accessed both eras through research and by engaging the memories of her parents, whose discussions evoked the 1920s and whose stories evoked the South.[26] Reflecting on the kind of discourse required for this novel, Morrison summons a vivid memory of a visual image from her own childhood: she remembers peeking into a trunk and gaining a tantalizing glimpse of her mother's life in the form of an evening purse decorated with jewels. The purse served as a visual analogue to her writing style: in *Jazz*, Morrison would create a language that would match its magnetism. *Jazz* was the first novel that Morrison wrote without the advice of her editor, Robert Gottlieb. She told Charlie Rose that she wanted to experience the writing process without the presence of Gottlieb's gaze. She would also write *Paradise* without any dialogue with Gottlieb, but would be reunited with him for her eighth novel, *Love*.[27]

In 1993, Morrison received the ultimate honor for a writer of literature when she won the Nobel Prize. She was the first African American writer to receive the accolade. Morrison has reflected openly on the political significance of the award: "It was as if the whole category of 'female writer' and 'black writer' had been redeemed. I felt I represented a whole world of women who either were silenced or who had never received the imprimatur of the established literary world."[28] She has since confirmed that the Nobel Prize has impacted on her writing life only in practical terms: she has noted a shift in attitudes toward her work, but the award has not changed the way she writes. Shortly after receiving the Nobel Prize, Morrison's house burned down. She has expressed her enduring sense of devastation at the loss of personal items such as photographs of her children, manuscripts of her work, and the view of the Hudson River that furnished the entrance of Beloved into her life.[29]

Morrison received the National Book Foundation Medal for Distinguished Contribution to American Letters in 1996. One year later she co-edited and introduced a volume of essays entitled *Birth of a Nation'hood: Gaze, Script, and Spectacle in the O. J. Simpson Case.* Her seventh novel, *Paradise*, was published in 1998. The third part of her trilogy, this novel examines the tensions at the heart of an all-black town in Oklahoma named Ruby. With its intricate nexus of narrative threads and large cast of characters, *Paradise* is often identified by readers as Morrison's most challenging work. Where *Beloved* centers on maternal love and *Jazz* explores the ramifications of romantic attachments, *Paradise* dramatizes the complex dynamics of man's love for God. The year 1998 also saw the release of the film *Beloved*, to date the only cinematic reworking of Morrison's fiction. With *Paradise*, Morrison was nominated for the first time for the Orange Prize for Fiction, an award specifically created to recognize artistic achievement in contemporary women's fiction written in English.

Morrison's eighth novel examines a further incarnation of love that is much neglected by literature: the empowering love that exists between children. The novel, entitled *Love*, was published in 2003. Morrison had reservations about choosing a title so freighted with facile associations. Only by limiting references to the word itself could she avoid its more trite connotations.[30] This was a strategy that she had employed for *Jazz*, making no direct reference to the musical form beyond the title.

Throughout her career, Morrison has engaged with a range of genres both within and beyond her work as a novelist. Her short story "Recitatif" was published in 1983 as part of *Confirmations: An Anthology of African American Women Writers*. The story explores the impact of racial politics on the friendship of two women whose racial identities are withheld from the reader. "Recitatif" has appeared in numerous short-story anthologies. Morrison's play *Dreaming Emmett* (1985) tells the true story of Emmett Till, a fourteen-year-old black boy who was beaten, tortured, and murdered after being accused of whistling at a white woman. The play was not published but was performed at the Marketplace Capitol Repertory Theater of Albany and received the New York State Governor's Award. Morrison has contributed to several musical projects, writing the lyrics for two song cycles composed by André Previn entitled *Honey and Rue* and *Four Songs*. She wrote the libretto for Richard Danielpour's opera, *Margaret Garner*, which premiered in 2005. She also wrote the lyrics for one section of an opera entitled *woman.life.song*, conceived and performed by soprano Jessye Norman.

Morrison has collaborated with her son Slade on a number of children's books, including *The Big Box* (2002) and a series of reworkings of Aesop's Fables entitled *Who's Got Game?* Some parents have voiced reservations about her children's books, in particular *The Book of Mean People* (2002) and *The Big Box*. In the former, Morrison gives expression to a child's internal questioning of various authority figures and in the latter she presents three children who live in a box because their parents believe that they cannot come to terms with the choices available to them; the parents hand the children everything they ask for, robbing them of their imaginative freedom. Morrison's children's literature poses some of the questions that are central to her novels: what constitutes "good" and "bad" behavior, and what is the true meaning of freedom? In 2005, Morrison marked the fiftieth anniversary of school desegregation in America with her book *Remembering: The Journey to School Integration*. Photographs recording the period of desegregation in schools are accompanied by Morrison's text; she taps into the consciousness of the children portrayed in the photos and gives expression to their thoughts and feelings through dialogue.

Morrison has made recordings of her novels for a series of audiobooks published by Random House. Critic John Young explored the purpose and impact of these recordings in his essay "Toni Morrison, Oprah Winfrey, and Postmodern Popular Audiences," where he noted that it is quite unusual for authors to read their own work for audio recordings. Always eager to find new ways to galvanize a reader's agency, Morrison sees this method of storytelling as a means of generating a new level of interaction between writer and reader. She told Robin F. Whitten of *Audiofile* magazine: "[h]earing the work requires a certain kind of attention and participation that is different from reading. It's a back-and-forth intimacy that true readers love."[31] Morrison was nominated for a 1998 Grammy Award in the category of Best Spoken Word Album for her recording of *Beloved*.

In 1998, Charlie Rose asked Morrison to name the achievement of which she was most proud. Responding in reference to her professional life, she pointed to her body of fiction. She also spoke about her work as Robert F. Goheen Professor at Princeton University. Morrison has taught at a number of institutions, including Yale University and the State University of New York. Her work at Princeton involved the creation of the Princeton Atelier, a program of workshops that gives students the opportunity to develop interdisciplinary projects with writers and artists. Morrison retired from Princeton in 2006. Just as some people were puzzled by her ability and desire to work as both an editor and a writer, others have wondered why Morrison would continue to teach after achieving such success as a novelist. In a radio interview in 2003, she told Tavis Smiley that teaching is "stimulating" and gives her a "way to stay current."[32]

DISCUSSION QUESTIONS

- Morrison has spoken of women in her family who "would run *toward* the situation rather than putting someone up in front of them, or retreating."[33] Which characters in her fiction emulate these different strategies and to what effect?
- Morrison has explained that many of her narrative lines emerge from images associated with her ancestors. In what ways do her novels reflect this kind of process? Do any of Morrison's characters uncover stories in similar ways?
- What do Morrison's novels suggest about the process of naming and its significance?

2

TONI MORRISON AND THE NOVEL

Toni Morrison is best known as a novelist. She refers to her major fictional works as novels and they are marketed as such. However, she does not align herself with the tradition of the novel form, using the term to define her fictional works only because she is a prose writer whose narratives stretch beyond the parameters of shorter prose forms. As Morrison has noted, the novel evolved after the Industrial Revolution from a growing need among Europe's middle classes for new, instructive narrative models; they required a literary form which would furnish them with neat moral paradigms and instruct them how to achieve certain goals. For Morrison, the function of the novel is not to instruct the reader through the elaboration of formulaic, end-determined narratives, but to illuminate and engage with social and cultural conflicts and do justice to their complexities. The novelist is under no obligation to furnish the reader with solutions.[1]

Since the appearance of *The Bluest Eye*, many critics have applauded Morrison for her innovative manipulation of the novel form. However, when she sees the word "experimental" in reviews of her novels, she questions this characterization and is quick to point out her engagement with the formal and structural conventions of black oral and musical traditions. One of the reasons that reviewers characterize her work in this way is because they are positioning Morrison as a postmodernist. The novel form has, of course, evolved over the centuries; as its subgenres have proliferated, it has moved away from its pedagogical agenda. Since the 1970s, when Morrison's first works were published, the form has been used increasingly as a vehicle for relativizing Western narrative models and registering their partiality through the incorporation of metafictional elements. The novel has become a more open and dialogic form, privileging multiple voices and discourses, defying generic boundaries, and rejecting the linear structures favored by eighteenth- and nineteenth-century practitioners of the form. However, it is misleading to view Morrison's manipulation of the novel as paradigmatic of postmodern writing. As Madhu Dubey notes, many of the questions and techniques associated specifically with postmodernism have long been the concern of African American fiction writers; it is reductive to regard their contribution to literature as "a subset of postmodern culture."[2]

"Metafictional" moments in Morrison's novels usually take the form of acknowledgements of her engagement with the oral and musical traditions of her heritage. In *The Bluest Eye*, the third-person narrative voice tells us that it must emulate the art of the jazz musician in order to gain access and give shape to the complexities of Cholly Breedlove's life, conditioned as it has been by trauma. One of the ways in which Morrison engages with the structures of her heritage is through her handling of closure. Traditionally, the novel is regarded as a more closed form than the short story or the poem. However, the "endings" of oral narratives passed on through communities and down through generations are provisional, as are those of jazz melodies. The final scenes in Morrison's novels constitute beginnings, often opening up new levels of apprehension.

The narrative poetics outlined and practiced by Morrison have led critics to question whether it is appropriate to apply the taxonomy "novel" to her major fictional works. In his reading of William Faulkner's *Go Down, Moses*, critic John Carlos Rowe writes, "Although in the popular imagination, Toni Morrison will continue to be hailed as a 'novelist,' she strikes me as a storyteller who understands the need for communal and collective tellings that will transcend the limitations and bourgeois ideology of the novel." Rowe goes so far as to state that Morrison's most famous work, *Beloved*, is not in fact a novel at all, but a "collection of stories."[3] He compares *Beloved* to *Go Down, Moses*, a text that was conceived by its author as a novel but was initially categorized by its publisher as a collection of stories. *Go Down, Moses* has been identified as a paradigm of the short-story cycle, a form composed of independent short stories linked through recurring characters, settings, or motifs. In many cases, the individual components of the cycle have already been published in their original incarnation as autonomous short stories. Morrison's texts are generally more unified than the short-story cycle; not all of her constituent narratives can be fully understood if read alone. Other taxonomies have since been suggested for the form that are perhaps more fitting for Morrison's fiction: terms such as "composite novel" and "novel-in-stories," which stress the unity between narrative components.[4]

The short-story cycle has its roots in the oral tradition and has been identified by writers and storytellers from a range of cultural matrices as their most representative narrative form. Morrison's novels share some of the properties and generate some of the effects often achieved by this decentered, non-hierarchical form: they are open narrative communities that challenge definitive renditions by privileging multiple voices and viewpoints; they elaborate stories through elliptical, discontinuous structures; they introduce narrative lines only to truncate them halfway through the telling, leaving the reader to wonder about the fate of particular characters; and they disrupt traditional, novelistic conventions of plot and characterization, making a subplot or an apparently minor character from one story the central focus of the next. Like many short-story-cycle writers, Morrison is often asked if she plans to return to the truncated narratives that haunt her novels: critics and readers of *Beloved* have expressed particular interest in the fates of Sethe's husband Halle, who was last seen traumatized in the yard at Sweet Home; Howard and Buglar, their sons who leave 124, disturbed by the manifestations of its ghost; and Amy Denver, the white girl who helps to deliver Denver. Readers of *Jazz* often reflect on the destiny of Wild, the mother of Joe, and the ten-year absence of Sula from the Bottom has intrigued many readers and critics. When she finished writing *Beloved*, Morrison spoke tentatively of the possibility of returning to some of its unfinished stories. However, when invited by Oprah Winfrey to become involved in a cinematic production of that novel, she said that she did not want the characters "in [her] house again."[5]

In *Representative Short Story Cycles of the Twentieth Century*, Forrest L. Ingram identifies the "tension between the one and the many" as the defining characteristic of the form.[6] As a composite shaped out of independent narrative entities, the short-story cycle embodies the possibility of asserting one's autonomy while engaging one's relational sensibility. It is this balance that is captured by the jazz soloist who improvises a new melody out of the various contributions of the ensemble. For many of Morrison's characters, this balance proves the key to a healthy, coherent sense of self. The dilemma at the heart of her trilogy involves finding and maintaining a sense of self-determination while experiencing intense love for another human subject.

Given Morrison's rejection of linear, end-determined structures, it is hardly surprising that she has little use for the structural conventions of the traditional novel. Indeed, she has revealed that she divides her fictional works into parts and chapters for the same reason that she refers to them as novels: "for the sake of the designer and for ease in talking about the book." For Morrison, textual boundaries are generally drawn toward the end of the writing process. The forms of Morrison's novels vary and are largely determined by their themes. In some cases, she manipulates her forms to embody the reality of her characters. *The Bluest Eye* tells "the story of a shattered, fractured perception" which resists coherent, linear narration and can be released only in fragments interwoven through a combination of third- and first-person narrations.[7] Looking back on her narrative strategy for *The Bluest Eye*, Morrison has expressed dissatisfaction with its execution. Toward the end of the novel, the fracturing of the central character's perception is captured in an internal dialogue; Pecola addresses a second self, seeking confirmation of her reinvention and her acquisition of the blue eyes she has yearned for. In the afterword, Morrison expresses disappointment in her treatment of the "silence" at the novel's "center." Looking back, she feels that she might have given this silence a form but that "it required a sophistication unavailable to [her]."[8] Morrison does however give shape to the splintered perception of Pecola's father, Cholly. In the first part of the novel, the third-person narrator presents us with a glimpse of Cholly's "rape," the trigger to his behavior as father and husband; it is not until the final part of the novel that we are given a fuller account of this incident. This discontinuity reflects Cholly's coping strategies: he must keep this incident at bay because even a "half-remembrance" of it can "stir him into flights of depravity."[9]

In her first two novels, Morrison generates what she terms a cyclical "rhythm." While the structure of *The Bluest Eye* is "circular," *Sula*'s form resembles a "spiral."[10] The circle figures a return to the point of origin and the spiral signifies a movement away from the center. The spiral image captures beautifully the dual sense of circularity and progression in *Sula*. At the end of the novel, Nel has clearly progressed; she has gained crucial knowledge about the relationships in her life and is awakened to the vital role that her friendship with Sula has played in shaping her identity. The final image capturing Sula and Nel's bond is a circular one: Nel's "cry" for Sula "had no bottom and it had no top, just circles and circles of sorrow."[11] Nel has progressed by circling back and reacquainting herself with empowering feelings that she has not engaged fully since she was a young girl. The novel itself moves forward while coming full circle: in the final "chapter," the narrative voice implicitly queries the pervasive sense of optimism about social progress in the 1960s, returning the reader to the terrain of the prelude, where the voice recalls the strong communal sensibility in the Bottom.

Morrison often manipulates the structures of her novels to question hegemonic notions of progression. In her fictional world, reengagement with one's heritage is often the key to genuine growth. This is the case for Milkman Dead in *Song of Solomon*, a novel whose rhythm resembles that of a "train picking up speed."[12] Morrison changed her strategy for this book, opting for "straightforward chronology" in order to give formal expression to a masculine sensibility.[13] The use of numbered chapter divisions certainly creates a surface impression of forward momentum. Structures are never straightforward in Morrison's fiction, however. In order to truly pick up speed, Milkman Dead must engage with the voices of his ancestors and recognize the value of entering into other people's narratives. Similarly, the characters in *Tar Baby* can move forward only by coming to terms with the past, figured in this novel by the image of the "afterboom."[14] In formal terms, however, *Tar Baby* is the most overtly sequential of all of Morrison's major works. The sense of linearity and forward momentum is compounded by the shaping of numbered chapters that often begin on a note of anticipation and end with a moment of revelation or with the tantalizing promise of further disclosure, propelling the reader forward.

Both *Beloved* and *Jazz* place a particular emphasis on telling as a means of personal growth. Through her active listening, Beloved inspires her sister Denver to reconsider a story which she has heard and told herself many times, awakening her for the first time to some of its circumstances and ramifications. Although Denver narrates and Beloved listens, they experience the story together, and the line between teller and listener dissolves. In *Jazz*, Joe and Violet Trace reinvent their relationship by recounting buried narratives to each other. The fluid forms of these novels accommodate this impulse to call and to respond; there are no marked chapter divisions and only textual gaps signal shifts in point of view and voice. *Jazz* marked a development in Morrison's handling of the relationship between theme and form. While the structures of her previous novels were crafted to "enhance meaning," the structure of *Jazz* "would *equal* meaning." She rejected the original opening sentence—a description of a woman "licking snowflakes from her top lip" while holding a knife—which, she felt, set up a suspenseful, causal structure at odds with the fluidity of jazz.[15] It is the anonymous narrative voice in *Jazz* that gives the fullest expression to Morrison's vision of a dynamic, interactive relationship with the reader.

Many critics have scrutinized this voice to show how Morrison engages the techniques of the jazz musician. In an interview with Angels Carabi, Morrison compares the strategies of the anonymous narrative voice to the musicians in a jazz ensemble: "Somebody takes off from a basic pattern, then the others have to accommodate themselves."[16] The anonymous voice in *Jazz* builds on the fragments of overheard stories while launching its own extemporized interpretation. Like the jazz solo, the narrative space is apparently boundless; there is plenty of room for expansive digressions on the beauty of the city's landscape or the intensity of romantic love. At the end of the novel, the voice acknowledges its contingency not only to other tellers but also to the reader, calling on him directly for further inspiration: "If I were able I'd say it. Say make me, remake me."[17]

Morrison structures her novels not only to enact a character's psychological conditioning but also to recreate a particular feeling or experience in the mind of the reader. While agency is always at the forefront of her vision for her readers, the means by which she galvanizes this agency varies. The neat structural demarcations deployed by Morrison in *Paradise* and *Love* are again deceptive. Morrison uses titled parts or chapters in these later novels both to illuminate and to undermine the boundaries that characters construct in order to define themselves or their communities. Narrative lines in these novels are continually suspended or truncated, countering the surface impression of self-contained, official stories. In *Paradise*, Morrison wanted the reader to experience the sense of disorientation and uncertainty of the stranger who enters a town for the first time.[18] She therefore presents the reader with a welter of fractured narrative lines; the reader must reassemble these scattered pieces of narratives by gleaning information incrementally from many different sources. Like the stranger in the town, the reader soon learns that no version is definitive, no matter how authoritative the tone of the teller. The act of reassembling prompts the reader to think about the very construction of stories, to replay events from different perspectives, and to reevaluate his own interpretations of narrative lines. For many readers, this means relinquishing preconceptions about the novel form and its purpose, a stretch that Morrison hopes to inspire: "I want to break away from certain assumptions that are inherent in the conception of the novel form to make a truly aural novel, in which there are so many places and spaces for the reader to work and participate."[19]

In all of her novels, Morrison aims to involve the reader by recreating the effects of oral transmission: the narrative itself must evoke the impression of an oral rendition so that the reader can "*feel* the narrator without *identifying* that narrator, or hearing him or her knock about."[20] One of the strategies that she uses to foster this kind of interaction is the inclusion of a "choral note" in her novels.[21] Morrison has identified the source of this note in her first four novels: the first-person narrator in *The Bluest Eye*; the communal voices of *Sula* and *Song of Solomon*; and the sounds and movements of the natural world in *Tar Baby.* The choral note remains an important component in the repertoires of her later novels and is used to particularly powerful effect through the personalized commentaries of L, the first-person narrator in *Love,* and the anonymous, first-person voice in *Jazz.*

For Morrison, one of the most important functions of the novel form is to alert readers to the value and relevance of the past. She uses the novel to engage with a variety of narrative structures and conventions, many of which have been passed on through the oral tradition. The title *Tar Baby* points the reader to the popular Br'er Rabbit myth deriving from African folk culture. Ever aware that the "word *novel* means 'new,'" Morrison uses the form in *Tar Baby* to engage new interpretations of the myth's meaning and associations.[22] The novel functions not only as a site for revising familiar myths and models but also for relativizing official accounts of historical contexts and events. Morrison uses the novel as a vehicle to scrutinize the many ways in which history has been reconstructed through misrepresentations, distortions, and omissions. While all of Morrison's novels acknowledge the currency of the past on a thematic and formal level, *Beloved* is generally recognized as Morrison's first historical novel. Its main narrative line takes place in 1873 and is interwoven with narratives and images that transport the reader back to the 1850s and, through Beloved's interior monologue, the Middle Passage. However, Morrison's novels defy strict generic classification. In a radio interview in 1987, she agreed with Don Swaim's description of *Beloved* as her first "historical novel," but she went on to note that it addresses concerns that remain pertinent to today's mothers.

While such categorizations can prove reductive, some critics have developed illuminating readings of Morrison's engagement with particular genres. Morrison objects to those associations that take no account of her heritage but recognizes fully her engagement with traditions such as the slave narrative, which she identifies in "The Site of Memory" as the "print origins of black literature." In this essay, Morrison writes about the functions of the slave narrative and delivers her analysis of individual incarnations of the form. She states that while "no slave society in the history of the world wrote more—or more thoughtfully—about its own enslavement, [t]he milieu ... dictated the purpose and the style. The narratives are instructive, moral, and obviously representative." She adds that early incarnations, which were framed by letters of endorsement and authentication from white abolitionists, were riddled with gaps because the writers were attempting to "make" their experience "palatable to those who were in a position to alleviate it."[23] *Beloved* has been classified as a postmodern incarnation of the slave narrative that gives expression to some of these buried issues. Writing in 1987, Morrison framed her novel with a dedication to the "sixty million and more" who lost their lives and freedom to slavery. While narrators such as Harriet Jacobs, writing in 1861, used the rhetoric of the sentimental novel, a discourse and form familiar to the white, female reader, to deal with sexual forms of abuse and oppression, Morrison's Sethe delivers a frank account of the devastating abuse suffered at Sweet Home.[24]

Morrison's novels are often identified as examples of magical realism or postmodern versions of the gothic, classifications that she finds particularly pernicious. In their many and various forms, these genres engage the boundary between the "real" and the fantastical or supernatural. The gothic novel has its roots in eighteenth-century Europe. It became a formal site for the engagement of issues generally ignored or marginalized by early incarnations of the "realist" novel. Writers of gothic literature employed a range of strategies to give expression to the fear and anxiety generated by confrontations with taboo subject matter: the fracturing of narrative voices and lines to undermine the boundary between the past and the present; the introduction of unlikely plot twists and interventions to point to a perversion of perceived notions of reality; the use of the doppelganger to query the boundaries of selfhood and embody the possibility of transgression; and the use of pathetic fallacy to reflect the sense of unease pervading the narrative. As a category, the gothic has expanded considerably over the past 200 years, partly owing to American engagements with the genre. In particular, writers from the Deep South have used gothic tropes and discourses to engage suppressed elements of American history. In "The Rise of American Gothic," Eric Savoy characterizes America's engagement with the genre as "paradoxical" given the national preoccupation with looking forward. America, "an optimistic country founded upon the Enlightenment principles of liberty, and the 'pursuit of happiness,' a country that supposedly repudiated the burden of history and its irrational claims, has produced a strain of literature that is haunted by an insistent, undead past."[25] Magical realism is a related but more recent category generally associated with the fiction of 1960s Latin American writers. Anne Hegerfeldt defines the genre as one that "incorporates, into a basically realistic world, elements which according to the standards of literary realism would be considered highly implausible, impossible, or even disturbing intrusions into another realm." While such interventions are "presented as though they are perfectly normal," there remains nevertheless a "tension" between the magical and real dimensions of the narratives.[26]

It is not difficult to see why critics have viewed Morrison through these kinds of framings. She has used the novel form to explore experiences that have been obfuscated or erased. Her novels query the line between the past and the present and the living and the dead and address issues that have been distorted or denied by official accounts of history. *Beloved*, a novel whose central figure embodies and helps the characters come to terms with the "insistent, undead past," appears in glossaries of gothic works and is often cited as an example of magical realism. Morrison has expressed unease with these kinds of categorizations because their founding characteristics have little to do with the musical and oral traditions that inform her narrative and formal poetics. These kinds of novels engage or interrogate boundaries between the supernatural and the "real"; Morrison draws her poetics from a culture where such boundaries and tensions have no currency at all. She tells Marsha Darling: "[t]he gap between the living and the dead and the gap between the past and the present does not exist. It's bridged for us by our assuming responsibility for people no one's ever assumed responsibility for."[27] In her fictional world, the dead can appear more "alive" than the living. In *Love*, May becomes a kind of ghost before she dies but the late revelation that L has been communicating to the reader from beyond the grave appears almost incidental.

Morrison has always used the novel form to ask questions: What do we understand by the words "love" or "paradise?" By what means should we attend to our past? How does one achieve and sustain a sense of self while living in a community? She aims to show us these questions rather than to furnish us with fixed answers through the elaboration of formulaic narratives. Again, the oral tradition sets the standard for her approach. Speaking of those narratives which have been passed down through oral renderings, Morrison stresses the redundancy of Western conceptions of the author as the unitary, totalizing source of all narrative lines: "[t]he fact is that the stories look as though they come from people who are not even authors. No author tells these stories."[28] Like the melodies created by jazz musicians, these stories counter the impulses of tellers and listeners seeking end-determined, unidirectional structures. It is this sensibility more than any other that has charged Morrison's fiction and influenced her manipulation of the novel form.

DISCUSSION QUESTIONS

• Morrison has stated that she aims to overthrow readers' expectations of the novel form. In what ways does she achieve this?

- Choose one of Morrison's novels and consider her use of repetition. Why does she choose to repeat particular incidents, words, or images? How does your reading change from one telling or representation to another?
- Compare the endings of Morrison's novels. In what ways do they undermine traditional notions of closure?

3

THE BLUEST EYE
(1970)

Morrison has stated that she wrote her first novel because she had felt the absence of a particular narrative in literature that she had read. Page numbers cited from *The Bluest Eye* are from the 1999 paperback edition (London: Vintage).

The novel tells the story of Pecola Breedlove, a young black girl who inhabits a world that offers no reflection of her beauty and subjectivity. Governed by the prescriptions of what Morrison has termed the "white gaze," this world projects its approval only onto those who fit its limited conception of beauty, a standard embodied by the child movie star Shirley Temple and Mary Jane, the blonde-haired, blue-eyed girl whose face appears on candy wrappers.

The first-person adult voice of Claudia MacTeer takes readers back to 1941, when Pecola was expecting her father's baby. Claudia and her sister Frieda planted marigold seeds to express their hope that their friend's baby would arrive safely. The baby died and the marigolds never materialized. Claudia moves further back to 1940, when Pecola came to stay with the MacTeers after her father Cholly burned down the Breedlove house. Seeing only revulsion in the eyes of onlookers, the Breedloves believe that they have a "unique" ugliness (28). Pecola prays every night for the blue eyes of Shirley Temple. Claudia expresses her hatred of the child star, noting in society's celebration of Temple the limitations of the white gaze. Claudia also recognizes her exclusion from white paradigms in the form of the blue-eyed baby dolls that she receives as Christmas presents, dolls that society presumes she covets and that she destroys.

It is through the narrative of Pecola, rendered by Claudia and an anonymous third-person voice, that Morrison dramatizes most powerfully the damage wrought by the "glazed separateness" of the white gaze (36). In reality, "[a]ll things in [Pecola] are flux and anticipation," yet she is defined only by her "blackness," which the white world designates as "static and dread" (37). Pecola confronts this dread every day. One devastating incident involves a local woman named Geraldine who has observed the script of the white world and absorbed its obsession with boundaries. Her son bullies the black children with whom he is forbidden to play and falsely frames Pecola for killing his mother's beloved black cat. Reading Pecola's skin color as verification of the little girl's guilt, the outraged Geraldine orders her from the house in disgust.

Before revealing the circumstances leading up to Pecola's pregnancy, the novel tells the stories of her parents, Pauline and Cholly. Pauline narrates parts of her story, describing some of its pivotal moments, but it is the third-person voice that reflects on their ramifications. Pauline injured her foot as a young girl and has limped ever since; when he first met her, Cholly kissed her foot, recognizing her vulnerability and loneliness at first sight. Marriage and motherhood did little to temper Pauline's loneliness. She sought solace in the movies, which exposed her to an array of formulaic narratives and narrow concepts such as romantic love and external beauty, identified by the third-person narrator as "[p]robably the most destructive idea in the history of human thought" (95).

Cholly is haunted by one particular encounter with the white gaze. The night he lost his virginity, he was caught by white men who shone a light on him, laughing and telling him to finish. Before transporting the reader back to this incident, Morrison presents it in fragments in order to reflect its hold on Cholly's mind. Marriage has an immobilizing effect on Cholly. One day he comes home drunk to find Pecola in the kitchen. He senses her loneliness and is overcome by his incapacity to console her. He sees her scratch her calf with her toe. Reminded of the first time that he saw Pauline, he rapes his daughter.

Speaking about the representation of Cholly's narrative, Morrison has stated that it was the first time that she'd written such a sustained piece without stopping: she estimates that she wrote his story in eight or nine hours (Stepto, 20).

Toward the end of the novel, we are introduced to Soaphead Church, a local West Indian fortuneteller, who measures status by skin color. When Pecola approaches him to ask for blue eyes, he tells her that she must make a sacrifice. He gives his dog some bad meat and when the dog vomits, he tells her that her wish has been granted. Of Soaphead, Morrison has stated: "I had to have someone who could give her the blue eyes. And there had to be somebody who *could*, who had the means; that kind of figure who dealt with fortune-telling, dream-telling and so on, who would also believe that she was right, that it was preferable for her to have blue eyes."[1]

In its final pages, the novel returns to the fall of 1941. Claudia hopes that someone will want Pecola's baby to live in order to "counteract the universal love of white baby dolls" (149). When readers next meet Pecola, she is talking to an imaginary second self, asking for confirmation that she now has blue eyes. Claudia closes the novel saying that Cholly died and that Pecola lives with her mother on the edge of town. Adults do not look at Pecola, and children who are not scared of her laugh at her. Claudia reflects that Cholly loved his daughter—he was one of the few people to notice her—but that "his touch was fatal" (163). Robbed of any sense of self or any language, there is no way back for Pecola, an unusual fate for Morrison's characters. Claudia tells readers that "[t]he damage done was total" (162).

The Bluest Eye is set in Lorain, Ohio, where Morrison was born and raised. She has spoken of her home state as a "curious juxtaposition of what was ideal in this country and what was base"; while Ohio seemed to promise freedom to black people, it also presented "some terrible obstacles."[2] Morrison captures this duality in *The Bluest Eye*. Pauline feels optimistic on her arrival in Ohio, but the hostility of some of the state's people leads her to seek refuge in visits to the movies.

In the novel's afterword, Morrison traces her engagement with its issues to an incident that occurred at elementary school, when she heard a girl expressing her wish for blue eyes; Morrison was aghast, wondering how the girl could fail to recognize her own beauty. This memory haunted Morrison, but it was the "reclamation of racial beauty" in the 1960s—manifested by public declarations that "black is beautiful"—that prompted her to write about it (Afterword, 167). Morrison wondered why this reclamation was necessary in the first place, and recognized the forces that provoked it.

In the novel, Morrison also exposes the impact of the white gaze on those who fit its paradigms and subscribe to its ideologies. Claudia reflects that the fear of marginalization generated in the community a "hunger" for "ownership" (12). However, the satiation of this hunger creates a different form of entrapment and isolation: those who manage to make their way into the mainstream are forced to do so alone. Geraldine is immobilized by her enslavement to the white gaze, constructing a world in which emotions are closely monitored and boundaries are fiercely guarded. Maureen Peal, a "high-yellow dream child," comes from an affluent family and attracts the community's approving gaze; however, she characterizes the lawsuits brought by her father as opportunities to "beat [people] up if you want to and won't anybody do nothing" (47, 53). Three of the most self-defining people in the community are the prostitutes who befriend Pecola and who show no concern with white conceptions of privilege, beauty, or propriety.

The threat of marginalization haunts *The Bluest Eye* from the beginning. Morrison opens the novel with a generic narrative that will be familiar to many readers: the first words of a child's primer, introducing the members of a white family. The words are repeated twice: once without punctuation and once without spacing. Excerpts from the primer appear throughout the novel, prefacing its narrative threads. Through this device, Morrison illuminates disparities between the primer's representations and the realities of life for black children. By running the words of the primer together, she shows the redundancy of this "definitive" narrative of childhood.

For Claudia, this sense of marginalization is tempered by the apprehension of her family's steady love, in particular that of her sister, which is as "thick and dark as Alaga syrup" (7). Pecola's sense of identity is more fragile because the impact of the white gaze has infected relationships within her own family. When an accident occurs in the kitchen of her mother's employer, Pecola's distress goes unattended as Pauline Breedlove rushes to reassure the mistress's daughter.

Morrison chose to open the novel in the autumn of 1941, before America entered World War II; the date signifies the approach of "something grim" (170). The 1940s were a time of hope for many Americans, as President Roosevelt's New Deal triggered recovery from the Great Depression. Yet few African Americans benefited from these changes. In 1933, the government established the Civilian Conservation Corps (CCC): its aim was to recruit young, unemployed men to save America's countryside. It has been estimated that out of three million available jobs, only 250,000 went to African Americans. The state of Georgia initially refused to admit African Americans into the CCC. In the novel, Claudia's mother rails against Roosevelt and the CCC camps. Henry Ford was widely praised for recruiting African Americans, but Mrs. MacTeer counts him as one of many public figures "who didn't care whether she had a loaf of bread" (17).

DISCUSSION QUESTIONS

- On Christmas Day, Claudia hopes "to have all of [her] senses engaged" (15). By what means does Morrison engage our senses in *The Bluest Eye*? You might consider her use of visual and aural images such as Miss Marie's laughter, the marigold seeds, and the dandelions noted by Pecola.
- Claudia describes her sister's love as "thick and dark as Alaga syrup" (7). What kinds of love does Morrison dramatize in *The Bluest Eye* and how do they manifest themselves?
- Morrison has asserted that "Language (saying, listening, reading) can encourage, even mandate, surrender, the breach of distances among us" while "[i]mage increasingly rules the realm of shaping, sometimes becoming, often contaminating, knowledge."[3] How does Morrison represent this distinction between language and image in *The Bluest Eye*?

4

SULA
(1973)

Speaking to Nellie McKay in 1983, Morrison revealed that she "has made women the focal point of books in order to find out what women's friendships are really all about." In doing so, she has pursued an inquiry which literature has largely dismissed: "Hamlet can have a friend, and Achilles can have one, but women don't, because the world knows that women don't choose each other's acquaintanceship. They choose men first, then women as second choice."[1] Page numbers cited from *Sula* are from the 2005 paperback edition (London: Vintage).

Morrison's second novel *Sula* chronicles the relationship between the eponymous heroine, Sula Peace, and her best friend Nel Wright, who grow up in a town named Medallion. They live in the Bottom, an area that was sold to black slaves because of its hilly, unworkable landscape.

When the novel opens, Shadrack, a traumatized World War I veteran, lies in the hospital. He is discharged and finds his way to Medallion where he settles. He becomes the founder of National Suicide Day, on which he marches through the town in recognition of the "unexpectedness" of death (14). Sula experiences this unexpectedness as a young girl. She lives with her one-legged grandmother Eva, her mother Hannah, and, for a short time, her Uncle Plum, another war veteran. Both Plum and Hannah die when Sula is young. Believing that her traumatized son will not recover from his drug addiction, Eva sets fire to Plum.

When her daughter Hannah accidentally catches fire, Eva tries to save her but is too late. Sula watches her mother burn and does nothing to help. When Sula and Nel play with a boy named Chicken Little, he falls into the river and drowns. The girls run to Shadrack's house across the river. When Shadrack sees Sula, he utters one word: "Always" (62).

In raising her daughter, Nel's mother Helene places a strong emphasis on manners and social conduct. She monitors Nel's "enthusiasms," thwarting her "imagination" (18). Helene has all but disowned her own mother, a "Creole whore," but when she learns that her grandmother is dying, she takes Nel to the South to visit her ancestors (17). Helene's mother enfolds Nel in her arms; when she returns home, Nel sees herself as an autonomous individual for the first time, rather than someone's daughter. This empowering insight gives Nel the courage to befriend Sula. Through this connection the girls begin to develop new ways of defining themselves: "Because each had discovered years before that they were neither white nor male, and that all freedom and triumph was forbidden to them, they had set about creating something else to be" (52).

When Nel marries, Sula leaves the Bottom. She returns ten years later, accompanied by a plague of robins. She tells Nel only that she attended college and moved around. Sula and Eva confront each other over the deaths of Hannah and Plum and Sula places her grandmother in a home. One day, Nel finds her husband Jude and Sula naked on the floor in her home. Jude leaves. Nel's sense of betrayal and bewilderment is rendered in the first person, the only time that this focalization is used in the novel. Sula sleeps with different men in the neighborhood, inciting the community's disapproval. She is disappointed when Nel joins the community in its judgment and is puzzled that they cannot share men as they have shared everything else. Only with a golden-eyed man named Ajax does Sula begin to comprehend the meaning of "possession" (131). Ajax leaves Sula when she begins to dress up and keep a home for him.

Nel returns to Sula when she hears that she has fallen ill and asks why she slept with Jude. Sula rejects Nel's moral standards and tells her that they will one day be meaningless. Before her death, Sula recalls hearing the word "always" and tries to remember who promised her a "sleep of water" with that reassuring utterance (149). When Shadrack sees Sula's body at the undertaker's, he remembers their encounter. The thought of Sula's death quashes his enthusiasm for National Suicide Day. This year, however, the community joins him in his march. Having been refused manual work on a new tunnel to Medallion, they march to the tunnel mouth to destroy the construction materials. Some members of the community die on their way down the tunnel.

In 1980, Morrison spoke of her particular fondness for Hannah Peace, explaining that this character has little sense of an "ego" and doesn't "impose" her values onto anyone else. In contrast to Helene, who projects her anxieties onto Nel, Hannah is "genuinely maternal" (Koenen, 69).

The novel makes an imaginative leap forward of twenty-four years. The Bottom's land has become an asset and white people have begun to settle there. At the end of the novel, Nel reflects on the fragmentation of the community and the isolation of its individual households. She visits Sula's grave and sees Shadrack, who feels that he knows her but cannot identify her. Nel utters a cry for Sula and recognizes their friendship as the defining relationship of her life: for years she has been missing Sula, not her husband.

Sula invites the reader to consider the pull of social boundaries and inscriptions, opening up conceptions of love and morality. When Hannah tells her friends that she loves her daughter but does not like her, the other mothers nod in sympathy. When Eva instructs Sula to get married and have children, her granddaughter responds: "I don't want to make somebody else. I want to make myself" (92). Ajax rejects Sula when she begins to don the raiment of the devoted wife, perhaps fearing the immobilization which Cholly experiences in his marriage to Pauline in *The Bluest Eye*.

Sula embodies self-determination by refusing to observe social codes and conventions. She asks Nel if being black and female aren't the same as being male. Despite the changes that occur during the novel's time span, Sula remains at odds with her context, untouched by those cultural forces which gain prominence as the century progresses. Owing to the absence of "ego" and "greed," Sula "felt no compulsion to verify herself—be consistent with herself" (119).

Morrison has stated that the novel's subject is "the question of evil."[2] *Sula* has been compared to a parable because of the prominence of omens such as Hannah's dream, in which she attends a wedding in a red dress, and the plague of robins that herald Sula's return. The parabolic resonance is compounded by the measured, restrained third-person narration that charts changes in the weather and the landscape: "Then Medallion turned silver" (151). Unlike most parables, *Sula* offers no easy identifications to the reader; rather, it problematizes moral categories. Sula tells Nel that "[b]eing good to somebody is just like being mean to somebody. Risky. You don't get nothing for it" (144–5). At the end of

Morrison has observed that Cholly and Ajax are similar in that they both "made up themselves" (Stepto, 19).

the novel, Nel recalls how her own response to the death of Chicken Little defied conventional morality and wonders why she felt some gratification in watching him fall. However, the novel does not invite readers to endorse Sula's views over those of the other characters. As Morrison notes, "[Sula] had a serious flaw, which led her into a dangerous zone": she is unable "to make a connection with other people."[3]

Sula opens in 1919 and closes in 1965. So far it is the only novel in which Morrison uses dates as chapter titles. In 1973, the year of the novel's publication, America officially withdrew from the Vietnam War, referred to by Martin Luther King Jr. as "the white man's war, the black man's fight." Those who returned from war seeking work faced further hostility and abuse from whites. In *Sula*, Plum and Shadrack return from World War I traumatized. Through these portrayals, Morrison debunks what she calls "history-as-imagined":[4] the official version of the soldiers' homecoming constructed largely by the media and dominated by images of triumphant white soldiers greeted by welcoming civilians.

In *Sula*, the bargeman rescues the body of Chicken Little only because he is a child. He immediately assumes that the child's parents are responsible for his death. The bargeman throws the body back in the water at the thought of the smell it will make. There is uncertainty regarding the racial identity of Tar Baby, one of Eva's tenants. The community refers to him as "half white," but Eva identifies him as "all white," insisting that she "know[s] blood when [she] see[s] it" (39). When Tar Baby is involved in an accident caused by the mayor's daughter, the police beat him and leave him in a cell in soiled underwear, contending that, "if the prisoner didn't like to live in shit, he should come down out of those hills, and live like a decent white man" (133). When Helene and Nel find themselves in a "whites only" carriage on a train to the South, they are berated by the conductor. Helene responds with her most disarming smile but the black soldiers in the carriage project their anger onto her. In Birmingham, there are no toilet facilities for black people, and Helene and Nel are forced to squat in the grass at the station houses.

The novel ends in 1965. Historian Hugh Brogan estimates that in the 1960s, half of the black population lived "on, or below, or near, the poverty line, the line below which, statisticians reckoned, their income was inadequate for the necessities of life."[5] In 1964, President Johnson declared a war on poverty, introducing a series of bills to regenerate impoverished areas through a number of projects; like the construction of the tunnel and the golf course in *Sula*, many of these schemes resulted in the further disenfranchisement of the black community. Throughout her fiction, Morrison both recognizes and raises questions about the impact of "progress." The final chapter of *Sula* opens, "Things were so much better in 1965. Or so it seemed" (163). Black people are employed in shops and schools, yet communities are losing their identity as family units become more contained.

DISCUSSION QUESTIONS

- "[I]t was a love that, like a pan of syrup kept too long on the stove, had cooked out, leaving only its odor and a hard, sweet sludge, impossible to scrape off" (165). Discuss the representation of maternal love in *Sula*.
- "[O]ne can never really define good and evil."[6] Does your reading of *Sula* sustain this statement? Which words or actions in the novel prompt us to question our moral categories?
- In *Sula*, crucial moments of awakening occur while characters watch each other in silence. What does each of these moments tell us about the observer and the observed?

5

SONG OF SOLOMON
(1977)

Morrison has described *Song of Solomon* as more "expansive" than her previous novels, its issues demanding a different kind of stage from the "enclosed world[s]" of *Sula* and *The Bluest Eye*.[1] Page numbers cited from *Song of Solomon* are from the 2005 paperback edition (London: Vintage).

One of the ways in which this novel figures the possibility of expansion is through its dominant motif of flight. *Song of Solomon* opens with a promise by a man named Robert Smith to fly across Lake Superior "on his own wings" (3). As Smith prepares to take flight, a well-dressed woman goes into labor and another woman standing nearby in a quilt sings "*O Sugarman done fly away*" (6). This refrain is repeated in various forms throughout the novel. The woman in labor is Ruth Dead, the wife of Macon Dead II, with whom she has two daughters, Magdalena Called Lena and First Corinthians. Their son, Milkman, is born the day after Smith's flight. The name Macon Dead comes from the two pieces of information that Milkman's grandfather gave a drunken clerk during the Civil War. Milkman is named by Freddie, the local janitor, who saw him nursing at Ruth's breast as a young boy.

All five members of Macon Dead II's nuclear family are estranged from each other and the wider community. Macon grounds his identity in his material wealth and tells his son that the only way to achieve autonomy is to own things. This assertion masks feelings of indeterminacy and

> In response to the suggestion that readers "don't admire Milkman's father," Morrison replies: "Why not? The people in these novels are complex. Some are good and some are bad, but most of them are bits of both" (McKay, 145).

alienation: surveying his properties at dusk, Macon feels that they are "in league with one another to make him feel like the outsider, the propertyless, landless wanderer" (27).

Song of Solomon charts Milkman's search for a coherent sense of identity. As a child, he longs for the ability to fly. Sitting between his parents in the front seat of their Packard, Milkman has eyes only for the "winged woman careening off the nose of the car" (32). When his wish is denied him, he loses interest in life. He works for his forward-looking father but has an abiding fixation with "things behind him," which finds expression when he becomes acquainted with his aunt Pilate, the woman whose singing accompanies the novel's opening scene (35). Unfettered by material concerns, Pilate lives in the woods with her daughter Reba and granddaughter Hagar. Pilate was born moments after her mother's death and entered the world without a navel. She deeply values ties to her heritage. She wears a brass box as an earring, which we later discover contains a piece of paper on which her father wrote her name, chosen at random from the Bible. On the wall of her house hangs a green bag that she never opens.

As children, Pilate and Macon witnessed the murder of their father by white men who wanted his land. Guided by his ghost, the children hid in a cave where they encountered a white man with a sack of gold. Macon killed the man and Pilate prevented him from taking the gold. When Macon returned to the cave years later, the sack of gold was gone. Now a successful businessman, Macon dreads the day that his white associates will find out Pilate is his sister. Milkman, however, senses his aunt's spiritual richness. After losing her father and brother, Pilate went to Virginia to seek out her mother's people. On her way there she encountered various communities but they all rejected her because of her stomach. This caused Pilate to reassess her life. Wondering how to discover some kind of value in the world around her, she decided to invest herself in authentic relationships.

Macon visits Pilate's house to warn his sister away from his son. As he leaves, he is captivated by the singing of its three women, hearing in their voices the possibility of the vital connections missing in his own house. As a young adult, Milkman experiences relationships as a pull on his latent sense of identity. He and Hagar become lovers, but he ends their affair when he realizes that he no longer needs to work for her love. Hagar, however, has been consumed by her love for Milkman and makes monthly attempts on his life. Milkman's friend Guitar is driven by his obsession with racial politics and is infuriated by Milkman's lack of focus. Guitar belongs to an organization called the Seven Days, whose members assassinate one white, whether innocent or guilty of murder, for every black killed at a white's hands. Guitar is ordered to avenge the deaths of the four black girls who were killed when a church was bombed in Birmingham, Alabama. Milkman, attracted by the definition of Guitar's scheme, agrees to help him find money for explosives. He will steal the green bag hanging in Pilate's house that his father suspects is full of the white man's gold.

The bag is in fact full of bones. Pilate tells Macon that they belong to the white man he killed: she collected them on the instructions of their father's ghost, who told her that you can never banish those you kill from your mind. Milkman decides to search for the gold, in the hope that it will enable him to build a new life. It is telling that Milkman, unlike his father, is unable to imagine the particulars of this life. When Macon contemplates the gold, he sees "[l]ife, safety, and luxury fan ... out before him like the tailspread of a peacock" (170). This image of effortless expansion is undercut when Guitar and Milkman see a real peacock and Guitar reflects that it cannot fly owing to the weight of its jewels.

Pursued by Guitar, Milkman travels south to find the cave. He visits the various sites of his family's past and hears stories about his ancestors. Having felt imprisoned by relationships with his father, Hagar, and Guitar, Milkman begins to apprehend the meaning of having "*people*" (229, Morrison's italics). He finds Shalimar, the birthplace of his grandparents, by chance. While hunting in the surrounding woods, he hears the crying of Ryna Gulch, a dead woman who was abandoned by her husband. Alone in the woods, Milkman is thrown back on his own resources for the first time in his life. Deprived of money, transport, and company, he is forced to look for meaning beyond the identity that he has constructed. He reflects on his stultifying relationships with Hagar, Guitar, and his father, and realizes that he has only partially participated in their stories, refusing to engage with their pain but expecting their love in return. Released from the forged identities of son, friend, and lover, Milkman comprehends his position in a much larger community, sensing the presence of his ancestors in the landscape.

The men of Shalimar tell stories about Milkman's grandfather, whose death signified "the beginning of their own dying" (235). One man recalls Milkman's grandmother, Singing Bird. One of her descendants, Susan Byrd, refers to Milkman's grandfather as "one of those flying African children" of Solomon, or Shalimar (321). When Solomon flew away to Africa to escape slavery, he left his wife, Ryna, who died of a broken heart, and twenty-one children. Solomon tried to take his son Jake (Milkman's grandfather) with him, but he dropped him; the little boy was rescued by Heddy, a Native American woman. Heddy had a daughter named Singing Bird, with whom Jake bonded and eventually ran away. Listening to the stories of abandoned women and flying men, Milkman is reminded of Pilate's song. The legend of Solomon derives from a Yoruba story of Africans who flew away from slavery. The story and the song capture the empowerment of flight that has long fascinated Milkman; however, they also prompt him to ponder his treatment of the women he has abandoned or disregarded. Before he leaves Shalimar, he encounters a woman named Sweet with whom he experiences sexual and spiritual fulfillment.

When Milkman returns, he discovers that Hagar has died of a broken heart. Pilate gives him a box of Hagar's hair so that he will have something of the person he killed. He tells her what he learned from a woman named Circe who cared for Macon and Pilate after their father's death: that the white man's bones were never in the cave to begin with and that it is her father's bones that she has been carrying. Pilate and Milkman travel back to Shalimar, where she immediately feels at home. They go to Solomon's Leap to bury the bones of Milkman's grandfather. As they prepare the interment, Pilate is shot. Milkman sings to her, "sugargirl don't leave me here," and tells Guitar to kill him, too. As he "wheel[s] towards" his friend, Milkman reflects that it is no longer important who dies because he has acquired new knowledge: "If you surrendered to the air, you could *ride* it" (337, Morrison's italics).

Milkman is surrounded by characters who are immobilized by passion or anger. In order to grow, they must see beyond their immediate context that offers little hope for expansion. The novel opens in 1931 and ends in the early 1960s. The men in the local barbershop discuss some of the acts of racist brutality that occurred during this period, such as the murder of Emmett Till. The men observe that Till came from the North but was murdered in the South and wonder if the murderers will be punished and if the media will even cover the story. The white newspapers ignore crimes against African Americans and lock black people out of any narrative of heroism, success, or hope. When Reba becomes the 500,000th person to enter Sears, she wins a diamond ring, but the local newspaper decides to publish a photograph of the white man who followed her into the store and won second prize.

Listening to the men, Milkman speculates on the possibility of forging a self beyond racial politics. While he finds an identity beyond these boundaries, opportunities for expansion are scarce for the women in the novel, many of whom are left behind by their vagrant men. The cries of Ryna Gulch resonate with the other women in her family, who will be abandoned in different ways. Macon and Milkman pay little attention to Ruth, Lena, and First Corinthians. Lena spends her days cutting up velvet to make rose petals; she tells her brother that she does this in order to sublimate anger provoked by his selfishness. She has spent her life trying to kill him in "little ways" (213). Corinthians, like Milkman, must shed some of the assumptions that have been instilled by their father. She believes that her good education, breeding, and yellow skin will secure her a man with a decent job and positive prospects; she deems inferior the women she sees on the bus. When she meets a yardman named Henry Porter—a member of the Seven Days—who compares her unfavorably to these women, she runs home, but on the threshold of the house she recognizes the nullity of her role within its walls. She returns to Henry, flinging herself across the hood of his car until he admits her.

Song of Solomon ends with an open, reciprocal exchange between a man and a woman. This possibility of reciprocity between the genders is captured in the novel's title, which recalls the Song of Songs, a book of the Old Testament also known as the Song of Solomon. A celebration of sexual love, it is the only book in the Bible to take the form of a dialogue between male and female voices. Although the identities of the voices are never confirmed, biblical scholars have assigned them to King Solomon, known for his riches and wisdom, and the Queen of Sheba. Critics usually identify Pilate as the novel's incarnation of Sheba, the woman who questions masculine wisdom.

The form of the Song of Songs enacts the possibility of finding identity through connection. Like the singing of Pilate, Reba, and Hagar, at times the voices seem to merge before reclaiming their individuality. It is significant that Morrison invokes the only book in the Bible that comprises a female and a male voice. Only through listening to women does Milkman learn how to expand. Of course, Hagar also requires this balance, as Morrison observes: "Hagar does not have what Pilate had, which was a dozen years of a nurturing, good relationship with men. Pilate had a father, and she had a brother, who loved her very much, and she could use the knowledge of that love for her life."[2]

DISCUSSION QUESTIONS

• "There's a male consciousness and there's a female consciousness . . . there are different things operating on each of the sexes."[3] To what extent does *Song of Solomon* sustain this statement, and what does the novel tell us about these "things" which act on the different genders?

- Speaking about her conception of *Song of Solomon*, Morrison has revealed: "I knew that I wanted it to be painterly."[4] How does she achieve this effect in the novel?
- At one point Milkman says, "They're not clock people, Guitar. I don't believe Pilate knows how to tell time except by the sun" (182). How does Morrison handle the passing of time in *Song of Solomon*?

6

TAR BABY
(1981)

Morrison's fourth novel, *Tar Baby*, is set in the 1980s but continues her exploration of the pull of the past. Page numbers cited from *Tar Baby* are from the 1997 paperback edition (London: Vintage).

The main action of the novel takes places on a Caribbean island called Isle des Chevaliers and follows the lives of those who live and work at L'Arbe de la Croix, its grandest house. The owner, Valerian Street, inherited his money from his ancestors, who manufactured candy. He lives on the island with his wife, Margaret, a former beauty queen. The butler and the cook, married couple Sydney and Ondine, live above the kitchen. When the novel opens, Christmas is approaching; Sydney and Ondine's niece Jadine, a fashion model, is staying at the house, and Margaret is expecting a visit from her son Michael. Valerian doubts that he will appear.

One night, Margaret finds a man in her closet and utters only one word in explanation: "Black" (77). The man, Son, has been hiding in the house, having jumped ship on his way to the island of Dominique. Sydney and Ondine, who pride themselves on coming from Philadelphia, are quick to draw sharp distinctions between themselves and the newcomer: Ondine is concerned that Son is black but not a "Negro—meaning one of them" (101–2). When Son greets Valerian with the word "hi," Syndey drops something; he has never done this before and thus betrays his unease at what he views as a disruption of the hierarchies not only of L'Arbe de la Croix but the world beyond its borders.

Son and Jadine fall in love but find that they are unable to reconcile their conflicting views of the past and its relevance to their lives. Son is most at ease with those who work at L'Arbe de la Croix and are known to its inhabitants only as "the Marys" and "Yardman": he meets them as Gideon, the gardener, Thérèse, the washerwoman, and Alma Estée, a young girl often seen at the house. Gideon informs Son of the island's heritage, telling him that it is named for a race descended from slaves who went blind at the sight of the nearby island of Dominique. The voices of the blind slaves can still be heard. The people of this race, to which Thérèse belongs, ride their horses over the hills and sleep with the island's swamp women. Gideon recognizes Son as one of this race. When Son tries to engage the interest of the household in Gideon and Thérèse, Valerian reveals casually that he fired them when he caught Gideon stealing apples. At this pivotal point, Morrison uses the technique of free indirect discourse to admit the reader into Son's consciousness. She retains the third-person narrative voice but replicates Son's mental language as he considers Valerian's exploitation of Gideon and Thérèse and his indifference to "the people whose sugar and cocoa had allowed him to grow old in regal comfort" (203). Annoyed that they were not informed of the dismissals, Sydney and Ondine voice their grievances to Valerian. During a heated confrontation, Ondine blurts out one of Margaret's secrets: she used to physically abuse her son.

Son takes Jadine away from this "pressure cooker" to his hometown of Eloe, Florida, but she cannot adapt to an environment that has strong claims on her lover. She is not permitted to sleep with Son and is visited in the night by a collective of women including Ondine and her own deceased mother. Jadine takes Son to New York, a city that can accommodate her desire for a provisional identity, but Son feels at odds with the urban landscape: he searches fruitlessly for the "Thérèses and Gideons of New York" (222). Unable to agree on a vision of their future, Jadine and Son argue. Jadine leaves New York and returns briefly to Isle des Chevaliers, where Ondine confronts her for failing in her duties to them. Valerian, after ignoring his wife for months, appears to have forgiven her. Michael did not appear at Christmas. Son returns to the island, where Alma reveals that she saw Jadine leave on a plane. She lies, telling him that Jadine had been met by a blonde-haired, blue-eyed white man. Thérèse offers to take Son to L'Arbe de la Croix in her boat. When they reach land, Thérèse informs Son that they are at the back of the island and that he will have to climb the rocks to safety. She warns him not to pursue Jadine, who has refused connections to her ancestors. The blind men of the legend are waiting for him. If he joins them, he will no longer need Jadine. Son reaches the shore and sprints on, "lickety-split" (309).

The novel's epigraph comes from St. Paul's first letter to the Corinthians and anticipates the conflicts that will disconcert relationships throughout the novel: "For it hath been declared unto me of you, my brethren, by them which are of the house of Chloe, that there are contentions among you" (1 Cor. 1:11). The characters disagree over the history of the island: Gideon states that it is named for the blind slaves; in Valerian's mind, the name comes from the Napoleonic wars and refers to the French soldiers traversing the hills on horseback; Margaret argues that there was only one Frenchman, so the name should be "Isle de *le* chevalier" (45, Morrison's italics). Throughout the novel, Son responds to the pull of his heritage, while Jadine resists hers. When Jadine tells Son her name, he responds with a shake of the head. As a "man who prize[s] fraternity," he calls himself "Son" in recognition of connections to his past and his authentic identity. In contrast, Jadine resents Ondine's demand that she recognize her identity as a daughter to them before finding her own narrative (283).

Morrison dedicates *Tar Baby* to a community of women: she lists five names and invokes "each of their sisters, all of whom knew their true and ancient properties." The novel is populated by women who assert their authenticity in different ways. When Son wakes up, he sees the women of Eloe, his hometown, emerging from their houses and welcoming him in. Jadine is haunted by an encounter with a beautiful African woman dressed in yellow who, upon meeting her gaze, spat on the pavement; this memory makes Jadine feel "lonely and inauthentic" (45). When she goes for a walk on the island, Jadine sinks into the swamp, which, according to legend, is home to the swamp women. She almost drowns as she resists their pull under the gaze of more women in the trees. The women, conscious of the centrality of their qualities to the world's creation, are surprised by Jadine's resistance to this opportunity for empowerment. The soldier ants that follow Son into Valerian's protected greenhouse are mostly women; in their community, males are called upon only at the queen's decree.

Descriptions of L'Arbe de la Croix hint at its provisional nature: "Except for the kitchen, which had a look of permanence, the rest of the house had a hotel feel about it" (10). The house continually closes in on

---

Critics have often suggested that the novel condemns Jadine's choices. Morrison denies this and asserts that the novel dramatizes the possibility of being a daughter *and* a "contemporary" woman.

itself as its characters strive to guard their secrets and stifle their grievances. Morrison furnishes the reader with a wider vision of develop-
ments in the house through her conjurations of the natural world that
surrounds it. Teeming with vitality, this world apprehends the implications of Son's arrival before the characters; the emperor butterflies
gather around the bedroom window and register their anticipation with
"vigorous flapping" (80). Of all the inhabitants of the house, Son is most
attuned to the inner life of this world, reviving Valerian's cyclamen
plants by shaking them and bringing the soldier ants into the closely
monitored environment of his cherished greenhouse.

Tar Baby abounds with broken and truncated conversations, as the
politics of race, gender, and class persistently assert their command over
the characters. However, the novel sustains the excitement of the butterflies by offering tantalizing glimpses of the possibilities that unfold when
relationships are allowed to develop outside of these ideologies. Valerian
experiences his most authentic relationship with a black washerwoman
whom he knew as a boy. When he announces the death of his father to
her, her silence and gaze awaken him to a new understanding of life's
possibilities: through her gaze and silence, he both grasps the gravity of
his father's death and comprehends "limitlessness" (141).

When Son and Jadine confront each other about their future, Son
draws from his heritage to explain his vision of Jadine's relationship
with Valerian. He refers her to the African folk story that relates Br'er
Fox's attempts to trick Br'er Rabbit through the use of a tar baby. Br'er
Rabbit outmaneuvers Br'er Fox, telling him that he is relieved to be
stuck to the tar baby; at least Br'er Fox did not throw him into the briar
patch. Br'er Fox falls for the trick, and Br'er Rabbit escapes to the
briar patch. Son casts Jadine's relationship with Valerian in this light,
describing a white farmer who catches the man who works for him
stealing some cabbages and makes a tar baby to trap him. By asking the
reader to consider the options presented to Son, Morrison adopts a different approach to the tar baby myth: through her revision, she asks
what kind of relationship would develop between someone like Jadine,
who has experienced the kind of advantages that mainstream society
could provide, and someone like Son, who emerges from the briar patch.
Morrison has given the following account of her appropriation of the
myth: "It's a love story, really: the tar baby is the black woman; the rabbit is a black man, the powerless, clever creature who has to outwit his
master. He is determined to live in that briar patch, even though he has
the option to stay with her and live comfortably, securely, without
magic, without touching the borders of his life."[1] Morrison does not
reveal explicitly which direction Son takes at the end of the novel, but,

like Br'er Rabbit, he runs across the shore "lickety-split," suggesting that he has chosen to return to the enchantment of the briar patch.

Morrison subverts the negative connotations that have become attached to tar in white appropriations of the story, in which the tar baby is seen as an instrument of entrapment. In Morrison's novel, tar is associated with expansion and mobilization. The skin of the beautiful African woman is compared to tar. When Jadine finally extricates herself from the swamp, she finds that she is covered in "a deep, dark, and sticky" substance (185). For Morrison, tar signifies "the black woman who can hold things together."[2] Several women stand poised to fulfill this role, and Jadine spurns the opportunity to join them: "The tragedy of the situation was not that she *was* a tar baby, but that she wasn't.... She could not hold anything to herself."[3]

DISCUSSION QUESTIONS

- In *Tar Baby*, meaning is often conveyed most powerfully through moments of looking. What do the characters learn from meeting the gaze of others?
- Morrison has stated that the characters in *Tar Baby* have "serious limitations, as all people do" and that they are "trying to come to terms with each other, give up a little something, behave properly. . . ."[4] What limitations do the characters betray and what must they give up?
- "'The Tar Baby' tale seemed to me to be about masks ... how masks come to life, take life over, exercise the tensions between itself and what it covers."[5] What kind of masks do the characters wear in *Tar Baby* and what are they concealing?

7

BELOVED
(1987)

In her fifth novel, Morrison examines the "undigestible" subject of slavery and its aftermath.[1] She has spoken of the "double-edged sword" of dwelling on the untold stories of those who lived through and died during slavery: the "horror" of slavery must be recalled "in a manner in which it can be digested, in a manner in which the memory is not destructive."[2] *Beloved* tells a story that defies easy articulation and yet must not be ignored. Page numbers cited from *Beloved* are from the 2005 paperback edition (London: Vintage).

The novel opens in 1873 with a description of a haunting by the ghost of a baby girl. The setting is 124 Bluestone Road on the outskirts of Cincinnati, Ohio, home to a woman named Sethe and her eighteen-year-old daughter Denver. Sethe's sons, Howard and Buglar, have fled; her mother-in-law, Baby Suggs, died after their departure. Sethe leaves the house only to work at a restaurant; the "serious work" of her day involves "beating back the past" (86). She is aware of the futility of this, as the briefest glimpse or slightest sound can evoke memories of Sweet Home, the Kentucky farm where Sethe was forced to work as a slave with her husband Halle, a Native American man named Sixo, and three men named by the farm's owner as Paul D, Paul A, and Paul F. In addition to Howard and Buglar, Sethe and Halle had a baby girl. When she last saw her husband, Sethe was pregnant with her second daughter

Denver. When the farm's owner, Mr. Garner, died, his brother-in-law took over. The slaves knew him only as "schoolteacher."

Two arrivals to 124 enable Sethe to confront the experience that she has been unable to absorb and to find a kind of release from her "knotted life" (114): Paul D, who arrives after eighteen years of wandering, and a young woman named Beloved, who appears at the house after Paul D, Sethe, and Denver return from a carnival. Paul D and Sethe tell each other their stories of the day they had planned to escape from Sweet Home. Paul D reveals that he and Sixo were caught. Sixo was burned to death and Paul D was tied up and forced to stand with a bit in his mouth. After sending her children on their way to Baby Suggs across the Ohio River, Sethe was subjected to a horrific attack. Schoolteacher's nephews beat her with a cowhide, opening her back. They held her down and stole her baby girl's milk from her breasts. She escaped alone, giving birth to Denver while on the run, helped by a white girl named Amy Denver who, seeing the manifestation of the beating, tells Sethe that she has a "tree" on her back (93). Halle's fate is unknown to Sethe but she realizes that he must have witnessed the attack when Paul D reports seeing him that day in the yard at Sweet Home, smothering his face with butter. Sethe tells Paul D that her first daughter died. Paul D also speaks of his imprisonment in Georgia, where he was forced to work on a chain gang. When they were not toiling or being sexually abused or beaten, the men were locked in cages in the ground. They escaped when a storm broke, turning the fields to mud. Paul D wandered from one place to another, witnessing the failure of Reconstruction, encountering "[o]dd clusters and strays of Negroes" seeking a place where they might be safe (63).

Beloved recalls no personal history, but her questions suggest knowledge of Sethe's past. Denver secretly identifies her as the sister who died. One of Beloved's most urgent needs is to feel connected, but her presence initially brings further feelings of dislocation to Paul D. She follows him around the house, asking him to call her name and touch her "'on the inside part'" (137). Paul D stays at 124 until a local man named Stamp Paid, who rowed Sethe and Denver across the Ohio River, presents him with a photograph of Sethe from a newspaper clipping. When Paul D shows it to Sethe, she must tell the story that has so far remained untold: the tale of the death of her "best thing," her "crawling-already?" baby daughter (178, 321).

After escaping Sweet Home, Sethe's contentment at 124 lasted twenty-eight days. On the twenty-ninth day, schoolteacher found her. As he approached the house with his nephew, a slave catcher, and a sheriff, Sethe gathered her children and ran to the shed. When the men entered, the boys were lying on the ground, covered in blood. The "crawling-already?" baby was in her mother's arms, her throat slit. The sheriff arrested Sethe and she was imprisoned with Denver for eighteen years. She was permitted to attend the burial of her little girl; in return for sexual favors, she bought a headstone with the inscription "Beloved." Upon hearing of the events of the twenty-ninth day, Paul D tells Sethe that her love is "too thick" and leaves (193).

Although Sethe delivers the most detailed account of these events, Morrison renders the story of the twenty-ninth day in fragments, describing them from several different perspectives, including those of Stamp Paid and Baby Suggs. Morrison also presents schoolteacher's response to the act in order to expose the full horror of what Sethe and her children would have returned to. Confronted with the sight of the boys lying on the ground, the baby girl with a slit throat, a woman whose gaze reveals that "something was wrong with her," and a baby whom nobody on Sweet Home could care for, schoolteacher sees only that "there was nothing there to claim" (175).

Beloved asserts her claim on Sethe in different ways, through manifestations of love and anger. When Sethe hears about Paul D's last sighting of Halle, she takes Beloved and Denver to visit the Clearing where Baby Suggs used to preach. As Sethe pays tribute to her husband, she feels the fingers of her mother-in-law stroking her neck; the touch strengthens until Sethe feels as though she is being strangled. Beloved tries to soothe her but Sethe stops her. Denver later tells Beloved that she witnessed her trying to strangle their mother. When Beloved hums a tune that Sethe sung only to her children, Sethe recognizes her as her daughter. Sethe feels relief that she no longer has to beat back the devastating memory of Beloved's death but feels compelled to explain her actions. Beloved responds with recriminations. As Beloved, who is carrying Paul D's child, becomes stronger, Sethe weakens. It is left to Denver, who has retreated from the community since hearing rumors about her mother, to seek help. When the local women hear about the events at 124, they approach the house, some uttering prayers. Later, some of the women report seeing Beloved standing next to her mother. When Denver's employer, Mr. Bodwin, approaches the house to collect her, Sethe's mind is flooded with memories of the last time a white man came to 124. She runs out with a knife and the women of the community restrain her. When they look back, Beloved has disappeared. Paul D returns to 124, where Beloved does not appear again. Paul D, Sethe, and Denver choose not to remember her, but her presence is felt in the novel's closing images.

Beloved is the first novel in a trilogy that evolved from Morrison's encounters with three true stories. Two of them—the story of Margaret

Accepting the Frederic G. Melcher Book Award for *Beloved*, Morrison spoke about the absence of a space where one could go "to summon the presence of, or recollect the absence of slaves." Thinking about the conclusion of *Beloved*, she stated: "I was finishing the story, transfiguring and disseminating the haunting with which the book begins... but I was doing something more. I think I was pleading for that wall or that bench or that tower or that tree when I wrote the final words" ("Bench," 44–5).

Garner and the photograph of a dying young woman who had been shot by her boyfriend—concerned a woman "who had loved something other than herself so much" and led Morrison to think about ways of "project[ing] the self not into the way we say 'yourself,' but to put a space between those words, as though the self were really a *twin*, or a thirst or a friend or something that sits right next to you and watches you."[3] When Paul D returns to Sethe in *Beloved*, he points to the possibility of this kind of self-conception, telling her that she is her *own* "best thing" (322).

When asked to comment on Sethe's act, Morrison has responded that she is not equipped to make any moral evaluation; the only person who can question the mother is the child who had no chance to do so. In the novel, Morrison presents Sethe's act as a way of reclaiming a role that slavery has denied her: the role of mother. The character of Beloved defies categorization, and the novel does not encourage the reader to dwell on whether she is the physical reincarnation of Sethe's daughter or a living woman seeking refuge from abuse from the outside world, as some evidence suggests. Morrison initially conceived Beloved as "a way of representing history, or the past, or a memory" in a way that was not "abstract."[4]

The reader gains fleeting access to Beloved's interiority in the second part of the novel. Morrison presents the thoughts of all three women at 124 through a series of interior monologues followed by a confluent conversation between the women; Morrison does not contain their utterances within speech marks, erasing the conventional boundaries that separate speakers from each other and the reader. Through *Beloved*'s fractured monologue, the novel meditates on the untold stories of those slaves who were abused and killed during the Middle Passage by the "men without skin" (249). Multiple voices overlap, clamoring to tell their stories. Horrifying images of drowning, abandonment, rape, and murder struggle to assert themselves. Beloved's personal story of severance from the mother is replayed as she strains to crystallize fleeting images of Sethe and to hear her voice.

Morrison has said that the novel form "should have something in it that enlightens; something in it that opens the door and points the way."[5] In many ways, Beloved fulfills this function by eliciting untold stories from each of the inhabitants of 124. Morrison has stated: "I know how hard it is to listen, and what's engaged when you listen."[6] In response to the loss of family members and estrangement from the wider community, Denver stops listening to the world. She has ears only for the story of her own birth. However, Beloved's active listening galvanizes Denver's fuller engagement with her family's past, prompting her to consider this story from her mother's point of view. Morrison describes Beloved's desire for stories as a "thirst," using the same image she employs for the second, "twin" self who watches you. Beloved's thirst for knowledge of Sethe's diamonds—the crystal earrings given to her by Mrs. Garner—turns the narration of this particular story into an "unexpected pleasure" (69). In response to deprivation and loss, Paul D keeps a lock on his "tobacco tin" heart (86). When he touches Beloved, the lid yields.

Beloved abounds with buried and truncated stories dramatizing the ways in which slavery assails any sense of self. Only at the end of her life, when Halle has bought her "freedom," can Baby Suggs begin to reflect on her own identity, wondering if she can sing or what kind of friend she would make. She offers the community spiritual counsel, urging people to find grace within themselves. Morrison dedicates *Beloved* to "sixty million and more," this figure being the lowest she encountered when researching the death toll of slavery. The novel reminds us of this staggering loss through sharply particularized images and narratives. Baby Suggs's quilt cover features no color, "except for two orange squares ... that made the absence shout" (46); local woman Ella, herself abused for years by white men, listens for the missing people in the fugitives' stories; Paul D meets a fourteen-year-old boy who lives alone in the woods with no memory of a life elsewhere; he also witnesses the hanging of a woman who stole some ducks, having mistaken them for her children; Sethe recalls the "permanent craziness" of Baby Suggs's friend, "Aunt Phyllis, who slept with her eyes wide open" and "Jackson Till, who slept under the bed" (114); she shares with Denver and Beloved memories of her mother who was hung, taking with her a "language ... which would never come back" (74); Stamp Paid finds a ribbon attached to a piece of scalp with "woolly hair" and hears in the voices emanating from 124 "[t]he people of the broken necks, of fire-cooked blood and black girls who had lost their ribbons" (213); he tells Paul D that he decided to give himself a new name when he projected his anger onto his wife, Vashti, who was forced to have sex with the master's son and whom he was powerless to help.

The threat of the white gaze looms over the characters' testimonies and their present-day experiences. After speaking with Baby Suggs on the street, Stamp Paid turns back quickly, aware that he is under the surveillance of a white face poised to pass judgment. Morrison does not need to specify the race of the four women for whom Paul D and Sethe step from the sidewalk to the dirt, nor the man who asks Paul D and Stamp Paid if they have seen "Judy," nor Judith herself who goes to work every day in the slaughterhouse. The Garners of Sweet Home preside over what Baby Suggs refers to as a "special kind of slavery"; Garner refuses to beat his slaves and allows the men to carry guns (165). However, he retains control over their identities, deriving his own sense of manhood from his treatment of his slaves and giving them guns in order to flaunt his Kentuckian credentials. Paul D is left wondering where his sense of masculinity comes from. When Garner dies, his definitions die with him. At the end of the novel, Denver is employed by the Bodwins, a brother and sister who campaigned for abolition and for Sethe's release from prison. Referred to as "angels" by Garner, they employ Denver at the suggestion of their servant, Janey, who must sacrifice time with her own family to work for them (171). Their oppression of black people is figured by the money jar in their home: a "blackboy" whose "gaping red mouth" holds money for "some other small service" and kneels on a pedestal bearing the words "'At Yo Service'" (300). Reflecting on racist codifications, Stamp Paid considers what they betray about their perpetrators: "White people believed that whatever the manners, under every dark skin was a jungle ... But it wasn't the jungle blacks brought with them to this place from the other (livable) place. It was the jungle whitefolks planted in them ... The screaming baboon lived under their own white skin; the red gums were their own" (234).

Morrison has identified Paul D as a "favorite character ... because he was complicated, vulnerable, strong, and he evolved."[7] One of the ways in which he grows is in casting off his assumptions about gender identity. Beloved unnerves Paul D because she seems to glow for no apparent reason; he believes that only a relationship with a man could account for her energy. His response to Sethe's revelation about the twenty-ninth day is conditioned not only by disapproval of the act itself, but by the discovery that he was not responsible for protecting 124 from the ghost: Sethe has not been tolerating life in 124 but has been living there because the ghost's presence does not trouble her. Sethe's escape narrative disconcerts Paul D and some members of the community who wonder how she managed to reach Ohio without a man's help. At the end of the novel, Paul D recognizes the kind of relationship that he can have with Sethe: the kind of bond that united Sixo and the woman carrying his child. Sixo describes the Thirty-Mile Woman as a "friend of my mind," telling Paul D: "[s]he gather me, man" (321). Sixo and the Thirty-Mile Woman sit next to each other without trying to usurp each other. When Paul D returns to 124, he wants to place his story alongside Sethe's. The novel ends with hints of Beloved's presence around 124. The closing images gesture toward her role as the representation of wider narratives; the narrative voice tells us that the footprints she leaves would accommodate the feet of an adult or a child.

DISCUSSION QUESTIONS

- "I wanted the possibility of this girl, daughter, grown-up, coming back into the house, to pose the important questions of the perfect dilemma."[8] What questions does Beloved pose and what do the responses tell us about the characters?
- Beloved is "looking for the join" (251). How does Morrison represent the possibility of connection in the novel? You might think about her use of imagery and her formal strategies.
- "[H]ow can I say things that are pictures" (248). *Beloved* abounds with powerful visual images. Discuss their function and their significance to the novel as a whole.

8

JAZZ
(1992)

In *Jazz*, Morrison explores the intricacies of romantic love and its ramifications for the conception and construction of the self. Page numbers
cited from *Jazz* are from the 2005 paperback edition (London: Vintage).

The novel's present-day narrative concerns a man named Joe Trace
and his wife Violet, who met and married in Virginia and joined the
Great Migration to the North. They came to Harlem in 1906. When the
novel opens, Joe has recently shot his eighteen-year-old mistress, Dorcas.
Violet has attended the funeral where she tried to cut her rival's face with
a knife. The novel charts Joe and Violet's attempts to make sense of recent
events. They gradually move toward a deeper understanding of their personal needs and, by the end of the book, revitalize their relationship.

Violet spends much of the novel reflecting on the kinds of love that
she has missed out on—she has no children—and wondering if she has
reached the stage where "everything is over but the talking" (110). However, talking in *Jazz*, as in *Beloved*, leads to a greater understanding of
one's self. Conversations with people from Dorcas's life provide Violet
with some illumination. She approaches Alice Manfred, Dorcas's aunt,
whom she eventually befriends. It is Alice who releases Violet from her
immobilization, telling her that she should focus on loving anything that
can be loved. Love manifests itself through telling. At the end of the
novel, the reader leaves Violet and Joe in a healthier state as they tell

> As critics have noted, in *Jazz* Morrison invokes the tradition of the "talking book." In *Loose Canons*, Gates writes about the centrality of the "trope of the talking book" to African American literature, observing that African Americans "had to represent themselves as 'speaking subjects' before they could even begin to destroy their status as objects, as commodities, within Western culture" (129).

each other stories that they have never disclosed before. The joy generated by this intimacy is articulated by the anonymous narrative voice that closes the novel by revealing that "*the kick*" is entering into a dialogue with the reader (229, Morrison's italics). These final words are an appeal to the reader to help the voice tell its own story. The voice calls attention to the agency of the reader by saying "Look where your hands are. Now" (229).

Joe and Violet Trace can make sense of their lives only if they come to terms with buried stories that predate recent events. They love living in the city because it seems to promise entry into narratives untainted by history: "[p]art of why they loved it was the specter they left behind" (33). However, fractured memories of dispossession and loss resurface persistently. Much of the novel is concerned with bearing witness to the experiences of people from their families in the South. The most mysterious of these people is Joe's mother, Wild, so-called because she lived in a cane field and its surrounding woods. Her absence left Joe with a vacuum that no amount of reinvention could fill. The histories of Violet and Joe intersect when readers learn about Wild's encounter with a man named Golden Gray, a figure known to Violet through stories told by her grandmother True Belle. When her mistress Vera Louise became pregnant by a black man, Henry LeStory or Lestory, True Belle had to leave her own family to tend her. The baby's "golden" skin and hair secured acceptance from his mother, although it took Vera Louise some time to feel any emotion toward her son (139). Golden Gray's complexion also won him adoration from True Belle, who, when reunited with her own family, made him the hero of stories she told her grandchildren.

When Golden Gray discovered that his father was black, he set off to find him. On his journey, he saw a pregnant black woman. His first reaction was to define himself in opposition to her: she was "a proper protection against and anodyne to what he believed his father to be, and therefore (if it could just be contained, identified) himself" (149). However, he questioned his judgment when he remembered his love for True

Belle. He wondered about the interiority of people he had dismissed as "nothing" but whose "absence was unthinkable" (149, 150). Golden Gray rescued the pregnant woman but did not wipe her face or try to see her eyes because he wanted to contain her within a stereotype: "She is more savage perhaps this way. More graphically rescued" (155).

The stories of Golden Gray, the child of a white woman and a black man, and Wild, the woman who rejects her child, represent deviation from social conventions. Morrison places these characters at the center of *Jazz*; to a large extent, real or imagined encounters with Golden Gray and Wild shape the relationships between Violet, Joe, and Dorcas. Just as *Beloved* turns on a devastating moment of loss, *Jazz* circles around one of Joe's memories: he recalls sensing his mother's proximity as a young boy on the bank of a stream and waiting for a sign acknowledging their bond. Only in the seventh part of the novel does Joe recognize the impact of this moment, realizing that he married Violet as a consequence of insecurity over his mother. Golden Gray and Wild have an enduring impact on each other. Reflecting on his encounter with the pregnant woman thirteen years later, Golden Gray recognizes her as "the girl who changed his mind" after he had resolved to kill his father (173). Wild is clearly affected by her encounter with Golden Gray; when Joe eventually finds the cave inhabited by his mother, he discovers the young man's clothes, neatly folded. Violet never meets the hero of her grandmother's stories, but her fixation on Golden Gray has an immobilizing effect on her. By the end of the novel, Dorcas's friend Felice has become part of the Traces' lives. Violet tells her that she could conceive of herself only in terms of a possible relationship with Golden Gray and that she had to release herself from this obsession in order to gain self-knowledge.

In *Beloved*, Stamp Paid hears the voices of the women in 124 and thinks of those "interior sounds a woman makes when she believes she is alone and unobserved at her work; a *sth* when she misses the needle's eye" (*Beloved*, 203). It is this sound that opens Morrison's sixth novel. It emanates from an anonymous speaker, but, like Stamp Paid, we feel compelled to listen. This effect is sustained by phrases such as "quiet as it's kept" (17), an expression the young Morrison often heard in adult conversation and that she used to open Claudia's narrative in *The Bluest Eye* in order to create a "conspiratorial" atmosphere (*The Bluest Eye*, Afterword, 169). In *Jazz*, perhaps more than any other novel by Morrison, the reader is able to "*feel* the narrator without *identifying*" him. The first-person voice relates fragments of the novel's interlocking narrative lines, but never identifies itself. Rather, it makes its presence known by commenting on its storytelling methodology, acknowledging its reliance on eavesdropping and speculation.

> Speaking to Robin Whitten about the publication of her novels as audiobooks, Morrison revealed that *Jazz* is the book she most enjoyed narrating. As Whitten described it, "she likes it best because of the run-on sentences, the arias and interesting dialogue, and a few 'pyrotechnics' she likes to do." Morrison also told Whitten: "I need to take a deep breath and almost sing it to get it right."

The voice becomes most effusive when speaking about the city. Morrison does not identify the novel's setting by name, but evocations and references signal Harlem. The main narrative takes place in the 1920s during the Harlem Renaissance, the movement of the "New Negro," recognized as a time of unprecedented creative output in New York City's black community. The novel's love triangle and its ramifications are played out against the backdrop of a city that promises exemption from historical consciousness and the possibility of instant replenishment. In 1926, eight years after the armistice of World War I, the people of Harlem are in thrall only to the present. As Joe and Violet approach the city for the first time, they dance to its rhythms on the train. *Jazz*, however, does not restrict itself to this narrative; many of its stories qualify initial impressions of the city. For Joe and Violet, the threat of dispossession lingers in Harlem; when they first move to Lenox Avenue, they face hostility from their neighbors with lighter skin. At the end of the novel, the first-person voice realizes that by investing in the romance of the city, it has missed out on the real stories of the individuals who live there.

Before the characters in *Jazz* can truly reinvent themselves and claim empowering new identities, they must come to terms with the losses of the past. As he looks back on his life of dispossession and forced reinvention, Joe states: "You could say I've been a new Negro all my life" (129). As Morrison has noted, the gaps and omissions in stories are as meaningful as the words spoken aloud or written on the page: "[w]hat is left out is as important as what is there."[1] Speaking about the Harlem Renaissance, she has commented on the way that this period in black history was appropriated by "the Other": "I'm not sure that [the Harlem Renaissance] was really ours. I think in some ways it was but in some ways it was somebody else's interest in it that made it exist." In *Jazz*, Morrison invites readers to view Harlem through a different lens; her concern is not the public figures of the Harlem Renaissance, but the "ordinary people."[2]

In *Jazz*, the narrative voice recognizes the pull of romantic love as "the thing worth doing," driving every human subject (63). It is this hunger, expressed through the persistent, unanswered declarations of Violet's parrot, which drives the characters to make skewed judgments. The desire to sustain the rush of romantic attachment provokes Joe to shoot Dorcas, whom he has designated his "necessary thing" (28); only love can account for Slim Bates's decision to allow his girlfriend to sing with his band, Ebony Keys; Neola Miller, the woman who reads psalms to Dorcas, bears the scars of thwarted love, holding the hand that had borne her engagement ring over her heart. Neola's warnings about the dangers of such love do not have the desired effect. Dorcas is intoxicated by the notion that a woman's instincts and emotions can be governed by love and passion, no matter the consequences for her sense of selfhood.

Dorcas hears in the city's music the possibility of entering into such an experience. However, the music, like the novel itself, does not limit itself to one narrative. Morrison does not use the word "jazz" at any point in the novel because she did not want the book to treat the properties of jazz as a theme, but rather to embody them in its form and structure. Jazz "symbolizes an incredible kind of improvisation, a freedom in which a great deal of risk is involved."[3] The first-person voice must improvise using the information it has gleaned to recreate the narrative lines of the past. Initially, the voice feels optimistic about this process—"it's not hard to imagine what it must have been like"—but is plagued by self-doubt in its narration of Golden Gray's story, berating itself for the limits of its imagination (137). Toward the end of the novel, the voice again chastises itself, this time for privileging its own view to the exclusion of others. Thus, it presents a coded warning to the reader about partial renditions of stories: "I was the predictable one, confused in my solitude into arrogance, thinking my space, my view was the only one that was or that mattered" (220).

Such admissions by the narrative voice provide the reader with points of entry into the novel. The book gestures continually toward the possibility of collaboration and connection. When one voice stops, another takes up its cue. The penultimate section of the novel is narrated by Felice, Dorcas's friend. Her last word, "pain," is taken up by the first-person voice that goes on to close the book.

DISCUSSION QUESTIONS:

- Morrison has stated that "*Jazz* is about the release of love."[4] What does the novel tell us about the different kinds of love that are available to us? How does Morrison give expression to the idea of "release"?

- The anonymous narrative voice presents itself as "curious, inventive, and well-informed," courting our trust while putting us on guard (137). What impact does the first-person voice in *Jazz* have on you as a reader? How does it compare to Morrison's other first-person narrations, such as Claudia's in *The Bluest Eye*?
- "Something is missing there. . .[s]omething else you have to figure in before you can figure it out" (228). What is missing in *Jazz* and what is its significance?

9

PARADISE
(1998)

Paradise opens in 1976, the bicentennial of America's Declaration of Independence, with a stark disclosure: "They shoot the white girl first."[1] The novel elaborates only on parts of this revelation. "They" are nine armed men from Ruby, an all-black town in Oklahoma. Ruby models itself on Haven, which was established by the citizens' forefathers after they were rejected repeatedly by communities in 1890. This first "Disallowing" was followed by another after World War II, which prompted the founding of Ruby. The location of the shooting is the Convent, which lies seventeen miles from Ruby and is a refuge for five women. The identity of the white girl is never revealed to the reader. Speaking about *Paradise* on *The Oprah Winfrey Show*, Morrison stated that she wanted to "signal race instantly" with this opening sentence and then "to reduce it to nothing."[2] By refusing to comment further on the racial status of the women in the Convent, she prompts the reader to confront the assumptions that he or she might project onto the story. Page numbers cited from *Paradise* are from the 1999 paperback edition (London: Vintage).

Morrison does not return to the massacre until the end of the novel. Bridging this splintered story are narrative lines involving the citizens of Ruby and the women who live at the Convent. Consolata has been at the Convent the longest. She was raped as a young girl and rescued by a nun, Mary Magna. Of her heritage, she remembers only the "[s]ha sha

> The reading of Consolata's encounter with this man as an engagement with a suppressed part of her identity is one interpretation. Morrison has offered several suggestions: "Is it a male version of herself she has reconnected with? A trickster figure? Jesus? Death?" (Hostetler, 198).

sha" of men and women dancing in the street (226). When Consolata was thirty-nine, she had an affair with one of Ruby's leaders, Deacon Morgan. She allows other women to stay at the Convent, but after the loss of her lover and Mary Magna, she retreats to the basement, drinking wine and wearing sunglasses. Mavis has left an abusive husband and is traumatized by the deaths of her twin babies, who suffocated when she left them in the car. Grace/Gigi was involved in the civil rights movement. When her boyfriend Mickey was imprisoned, she headed for Ruby after hearing about a landmark of two entwined trees; sitting between them would generate an unimaginable "ecstasy" (66). Gigi has an affair with K.D., the heir to the Morgan legacy. Seneca finds refuge in the Convent from a history of abandonment and sexual abuse that has caused her to self-harm. The last to arrive is Pallas, or Divine, who has been betrayed by her mother and boyfriend. She ran away and, it is implied, was raped by a group of men.

It is Consolata's story that we encounter last, bringing us to the days leading up to the massacre. After emerging from the basement, she experiences an awakening that unlocks her from her malaise. She is approached by a man; when they address each other, she suddenly finds that he is standing beside her but does not seem to have moved. When the man removes his hat and sunglasses, he is described in the terms that we associate with Consolata: he has "tea-colored hair" and eyes "as round and green as new apples" (252). Telling Consolata that she knows who he is, the man perhaps embodies the idea of the "twin" self posited by Morrison in her conversation with Gloria Naylor.

After this encounter, Consolata addresses the women in the Convent. She tells them to lie down on the floor and she traces the outline of each woman's body. In a scene reminiscent of *Beloved* when Sethe locks the door of 124, shutting out the rest of the world and leaving the three women within its walls "free at last to be what they liked" (*Beloved*, 235), the Convent women paint their lives and share their stories. Consolata conjures the image of a paradisal space, and the women dance and create an open, uncensored narrative community, where they give voice to "half-formed" and "never-dreamed" tales (264).

When the men attack the Convent, the "white girl" is shot down. Consolata appears and sees her old lover, Deacon, and states: "You're back" (289). Deacon reflects later that she was not addressing him, but a presence hovering above him. Deacon tries to stop his brother Steward from shooting Consolata but is unsuccessful. Her last word is "Divine" (291). The men think that they have shot the other women through the windows but find no evidence of this. The town gets to work to establish a definitive narrative of the massacre in which the attack is initiated by the women. When the minister Richard Misner and his companion Anna Flood visit the Convent, they find no bodies, but Anna feels the presence of a raised window and Richard sees a door in the open air outside the Convent.

After witnessing the death of Consolata, Deacon Morgan approaches Misner and experiences his first open dialogue. Steward focuses his attention on his nephew. Most of the citizens of Ruby believe that the men are guilty of a crime but deem the absence of direct consequence—the deaths of the women are never investigated—as a reprieve. However, the townspeople must recognize for the first time a loss that they cannot attribute to historical forces or to the Convent: the death of Save-Marie, the daughter of one of Ruby's founding families. The absence of the Convent women continues to haunt the town. One of Ruby's marginalized women, Billie Delia, senses their presence and wonders not if but "[w]hen" they will come back (308). In *Paradise*, as in Morrison's other novels, the dead are part of the order of things: Mavis hears the laughter of twins Merle and Perle in the Convent; the dead sons of Soane and Deacon communicate with their mother; in a burned-out farmhouse, Consolata and Deacon see the "[n]ether shapes" of the family who perished there (233). At the end of the novel, the Convent women appear to members of their families. The book closes with the image of Consolata in her own paradisal space, where she experiences "the unambivalent bliss of going home to be at home" (318).

Ruby claims its legacy of dispossession and reinvention as its defining narrative: as such, it informs not only the town's sense of its past, but also its vision of its future. The men of Ruby monitor closely its population, inverting the racial hierarchy that operates "Out There." Speaking about the novel, Morrison has observed that "isolation carries the seeds of its own

Morrison usually knows the endings of her novels from the outset, but not the openings. *Paradise* is the exception. As she revealed to Charlie Rose in 1998, she had a strong sense of the opening of this novel at the start of the writing process, but not the end.

destruction."[3] "Deafened by the roar of its own history," Ruby excludes other discourses so that the words "outsider" and "enemy" become interchangeable (306, 212). Morrison counters Ruby's narrow vision by dramatizing stories that have been written out of its history and placing them alongside the town's dominant narrative. *Paradise* is the first of her novels to identify "chapters" with individual titles rather than a date, a number, or a gap in the text. The chapters take the names of those women whose stories have been edited or distorted. Two of these women come from Ruby: as the daughter of Roger Best, "the first to violate the blood rule," Patricia senses the denial of full acceptance (195); as a baby, Lone DuPres was taken in by one of Ruby's women. Questions about her parentage confine her to the town's margins. The final chapter is named for Save-Marie.

As always, Morrison's readers must look for meaning beyond textual boundaries. The women's stories are not contained within their designated chapters, but are dispersed across the text. Readers learn about the tree formation in the chapter entitled "Gigi," but have to wait until Consolata's chapter to see its effect. This scattering counters the ethos of Ruby's founder, Zechariah Morgan, who dreads the dispersal of his people: "He would not have had trouble imagining the scariness of having everybody he knew thrown apart, thrown into different places in a foreign land and becoming alien to each other" (192). The novel's form counters the patriarchal ideology of the town; the experiences of Ruby's men are contained within the frames of the women's stories.

During a conversation between Consolata and Deacon's wife Soane, "a gander scream[s] in the yard, scattering the geese before him" (246). This striking image captures the gender politics of Ruby and prefigures the fragmentation of the female community at the Convent. Ruby's men project any fears of destabilization onto women, designating female sexuality as the site of potential deviation. Deacon and Steward Morgan base their paradigm of womanhood on an image they shared during their youth: the sight of nineteen nameless, smiling "Negro ladies" laughing and posing for a photograph (109). Their sister Ruby, for whom the town is named, died in childbirth but has come to embody this ideal in the town's imagination. Those women who deviate from this ideal are designated a threat: the fairer-skinned women of the Best family and Consolata, whose tea-brown skin fascinates Deacon. In Ruby, female sexuality and morality are inextricably linked: Deacon reflects that his wife is "as beautiful as it was possible for a good woman to be" and expresses incredulity at Consolata's beauty (112).

Some women are recognized as legitimate members of the community. However, their sense of identity hinges on the men they are allowed to marry and the town offers few outlets for their private thoughts and desires. The ramifications of Ruby's gender ideology emerge not only in relations between the genders, but also in relations between the town's men. Commenting on masculine discourse, Morrison has stated: "Men can hide easier because they can always be men. They can be abstract.... They have an idea of how to be male and they talk about it a lot. I'm not sure that they talk to each other about the other thing, personal identity."[4] As a safeguard against self-interrogation, the men of Ruby recount the stories of their ancestors; they do not regard their own lives as material for narration. Until he approaches Misner, Deacon's exchanges with men are limited to "wordless ones with his brother or brandishing ones with male companions" (301). Moments of self-examination are arrested as unpalatable feelings rise to the surface and are projected onto women. Harper Jury's attempts at self-analysis give way to reflections on the dangers of women.

The women counter these projections by becoming the guardians of stories that are deemed a threat to the town's unanimity. Patricia is Ruby's self-designated chronicler. Listening to the women's conversations in Ruby, she becomes enlightened to the town's secret history. Among Ruby's buried stories are those that involve engagement with the women of the Convent: Billie Delia, a young woman erroneously suspected of promiscuity, seeks sanctuary there; Soane Morgan, aware that her husband is having an affair, asks Consolata to relieve her of the prospect of a third child; Sweetie Fleetwood, the devoted mother of sick children ignored by the Fleetwood men, goes to the Convent for relief from the burdens of caring.

Consolata's inclusive vision debunks Ruby's polarized characterizations of women as embodiments of sexuality or purity. She speaks to the women in the Convent about the relationship *between* Eve and Mary, discarding the categorizations that have framed these women throughout history. Her words echo those of Lone DuPres, who first perceives Consolata's ability to enter people's souls and heal them. Consolata expresses ambivalence about this ability, but Lone tells her to look beyond the prescriptions of organized religion: she must not "unbalance" the world by distinguishing it from its creator (244).

Living in a town that is preoccupied with replication, the citizens of Ruby cultivate an unhealthy kind of division in order to secure their place in the community and attend to deviant personal needs. The Convent is a site for an empowering kind of duality. The unidentified man who approaches Consolata functions as a questioning, relativizing twin self. When Seneca leads Pallas through the Convent for the first time, the new arrival senses that "she might meet herself here—an unbridled, authentic self, but which she thought of as a 'cool' self—in one of the house's many rooms" (177). Outside the Convent, Dovey, Steward's wife, experiences a similar kind of connection with a male "Friend" to whom she tells "[t]hings she didn't know were on her mind"; her acceptance of her Friend as "hers alone" suggests that she recognizes this presence as an embodiment of her submerged self, which tacitly queries Ruby's values (92). It is telling that, in the cases of Consolata and Dovey, these second selves take the form of men, suggesting the possibility of honest communication between the genders.

Paradise is the third part of Morrison's trilogy and explores the complexities involved in loving God. Speaking about Ruby's citizens, she states: "[t]hese people really believe that their lives are structured by and glorified by God ... I wanted to try to describe that and try to describe how that love can go awry."[5] Ruby's definitive narrative is told from the "pulpit" (188). While searching for a home, the men of Haven carried an oven bearing the motto "Beware the Furrow of His Brow." The older members of Ruby model their identities on the motto which is, Harper tells the community, code for: "'Look out. The power is mine. Get used to it'" (87). Ruby's younger generation wants to change the message to reflect their burgeoning sense of empowerment: "Be the Furrow of His Brow." The entrenchment of Ruby's religious ideology emerges in the cast list of its nativity play, which features fewer families each year that it is performed.

Other "chink[s]" and "crack[s]" in Ruby's partial story testify to the influence of those external, historical forces from which the leaders claim immunity (112). Some of the new tensions pervading Ruby are a reflection of issues raised by the black nationalist movement that emerged in the 1960s and 1970s. Richard Misner, the town's progressive minister, meets resistance when he endorses engagement with African heritage as a means of empowerment. Unlike the founders of Ruby, Misner recognizes the influence of events in the wider world; he reflects that much of the unrest in the town stems from the murder of Martin Luther King Jr. When the citizens of Ruby refer to social or historical contexts, they do so only to account for aberrant behavior or death: while the men of the town attribute Menus's drinking habits to experiences in Vietnam, Patricia remembers that they forced him to send home the "sandy-haired girl" he had wanted to marry (195). Until the death of Save-Marie, the only death that the town has acknowledged is that of its namesake; anyone else who perishes does so at the hands of history alone.

DISCUSSION QUESTIONS

- "From the beginning, its people were free and protected" (8). What constitutes freedom for the various characters in *Paradise*?

• Consider the representation of Billie Delia. What role does she play in the novel?

• Speaking about *Paradise*, Morrison has stated that she "wanted to force the reader to become acquainted with the communities" and to replicate the experience of "walk[ing] into a neighborhood."[6] What methods does she use to achieve this effect?

10

LOVE
(2003)

Morrison's eighth novel explores a further variation of love: that which is shared by children. The italicized commentary of a woman named L, which stands for Love, frames the novel and provides a coda to some of its parts. L used to be the chef at a seaside resort owned by a man named Bill Cosey. She traces the history of the resort in her opening commentary, telling us that it was constructed in the 1930s as "*a playground for folk who felt the way he did, who studied ways to contradict history.*"[1] Converted during the Depression, the resort became the "best and best-known vacation spot for colored folk on the East Coast," but the 1950s and 1960s brought new conditions, and people began to opt for the Hilton or cruise ships (6). Morrison has spoken about the context of *Love* as a "period ... that has been reduced to a very simple story. Rosa Parks. Martin Luther King. Everybody jumped on the train, hard work, some battles, it all came out fine ... a story of progress." While assimilation was "great," she wanted to explore some of its attendant losses in *Love*.[2]

Page numbers cited from *Love* are from the 2004 paperback edition (London: Vintage).

In the 1990s, Cosey's resort is no longer a destination but a stop-off point for commuters. Characters in the novel offer different reasons for this demise: a hurricane, Cosey's behavior, and the impact of integration, which drove many of the resort's upwardly mobile clientele to other

> Junior is an incarnation of the "outlaw" figure that has always interested Morrison. She describes Junior as a "poor, rootless, free-floating young woman—a survivor, a manipulator, a hungry person," but adds: "she does create a space where people can come with their better selves" (Houston, 230).

destinations. When the novel opens, only the youngest members of the family are alive: Cosey's granddaughter Christine and his second wife Heed. Heed was Christine's best friend until Cosey bought her from her destitute family for two hundred dollars to be his bride. She was eleven years old. Christine and Heed now live in the house that Cosey apparently left to his "sweet Cosey child" in a will, which was hastily written on a menu. This ambiguous wording has provoked an ongoing battle between the women. Heed plans to forestall Christine's attempts to take the house and employs a young woman, Junior, to assist her. Junior is fascinated by the portrait of Bill Cosey on Heed's wall and has an affair with Romen, a local boy who also works for Heed.

The novel moves backward and forward in time, revisiting pivotal encounters between the characters and unveiling secret gestures and connections: Heed's affair with a hotel guest, Sinclair; L's forging of the will on a menu to ensure protection for the Cosey women; Cosey's ongoing relationship with Celestial, a prostitute and the recipient of his original will; the burial of the hotel deed by Cosey's daughter-in-law May. Seeking definition outside of the Cosey family, Christine leaves the resort as a young woman and joins the black nationalist movement. Involvement in the movement becomes an outlet for her personal needs and grievances. However, her enthusiasm diminishes by 1970, when it is "sapped by funerals" (163–4). The gender ideology of the movement is called into question when Christine's boyfriend Fruit refuses to act on the rape of a student volunteer: "The girl's violation carried no weight against the sturdier violation of male friendship" (166).

The novel also takes us back to the misunderstandings that further estranged the two girls after Heed's marriage: Heed returns from her honeymoon desperate to tell Christine of all that she has seen but is greeted with scornful laughter at her new clothes; she makes a peace offering of her wedding ring to Christine, who calls her a slave; when Christine corrects Heed's grammar and Cosey spanks his wife, Heed sets fire to Christine's bedroom; at Cosey's funeral, Heed stops Christine from placing rings on her husband's fingers and screams "in recognition that she would never hear the word [love] again" (130). At the end of the novel,

Morrison unveils the most devastating day in the lives of the girls: the day when Bill Cosey touched Heed for the first time and when Christine saw him masturbating in her bedroom. Neither girl could express her sense of shame. When Heed found Christine on that day, she saw that her friend had vomited and read this as a reaction to her own humiliation.

Heed does not return to the hotel until the end of the novel. In the attic, she instructs Junior to forge a will leaving everything unequivocally to her. Christine arrives at the hotel, and as the women confront each other, Junior stealthily pulls the carpet under Heed's feet. The floorboards give way, and Heed falls. Christine instinctively goes to save her while Junior flees the scene. For the first time since Heed's marriage, the women talk honestly. Heed reveals that she married Cosey to be near Christine; Christine tells Heed that she wanted to go on her honeymoon with her. When Junior tells Romen what has occurred, he leaves her to help the two old women. By the end of the novel, we know that one of the women has died.

Although Cosey tries to defy history, social and racial boundaries remain entrenched in his world. Local women unite in laughter over Cosey's choice of Heed, whom they dismiss as "sort of physical ... [y]ou know, jungle-y" (75). Cosey's choice is the only point on which Christine and her mother May concur. They have conflicting ideas about racial politics but agree in their identification of Heed as "*the throwback they both had fought*" (141). L views much of Cosey's behavior as a reaction against his father. Known to the black community as Dark, he was a courthouse informer who colluded with the police. While Cosey tries to take the opposite action to his father, the people of the local community know that they aren't supposed to frequent the hotel as guests or make use of its facilities. By the 1950s, the resort is vulnerable to the most sinister threats from the outside world, figured in L's commentary by the "*Police-heads*" who appear one morning in 1958 "*like a posse*": "*dirty things with big hats who shoot up out of the ocean to harm loose women and eat disobedient children*" (5).

The voice of L meditates at length on some of love's many forms: unlike the anonymous narrative voice in *Jazz*, she aims to counter the emphasis on erotic "*infatuation*" that "*leaps over anything, takes the biggest chair, the largest slice, rules the ground wherever it walks, from a mansion to a swamp*" (63). L prefers to dwell on other kinds of love, such as the love between children. As Sula and Nel found in *Sula*, it is a potentially liberating love because it is untainted by societal expectations. Romen performs two of the novel's great acts of love. In her opening commentary, L expresses wonder that her people have "*forgotten the beauty of meaning much by saying little*" (3). Romen's love manifests itself through quiet acts of protection. He foregoes his reputation among his friends to rescue a girl from a gang rape and overlooks his infatuation with Junior to attend to Heed and Christine at the end of the novel. In the first instance, he does not even realize that he is rescuing the girl, but watches his own hands as they approach the headboard to untie her. L's commentary also provides important insights into the novel's many "half-told" stories, such as Cosey's pivotal choice of Heed as his bride, which she attributes to a desire to *"make old Dark groan"* (139). L keeps some of her most potent secrets until the novel's end, when readers discover that it was she who poisoned Cosey, buried his original will that left everything to Celestial, and forged the menu to ensure that the Cosey women were cared for. Only when Heed and Christine talk of missing L do readers realize that she has been narrating from beyond the grave.

Bill Cosey is represented in a number of ways throughout the novel as a "prince" (37); the "county's role model" (37); an entrepreneur; a "bourgeois traitor" (163); a conjuror of a "counterfeit world" (111); the "Big Man who, with no one to stop him, could get away with it and anything else he wanted" (133); and *an ordinary man ripped, like the rest of us, by wrath and love"* (200). All of the women in the novel are connected to Cosey in some way. They have, to varying degrees, grounded their identities in their relationships with him. The chapters in the novel are named for the various roles that Cosey plays in the women's lives. As in *Paradise*, patriarchal domination is countered by moments of connection between the female characters. One of the most resonant connections arises from Christine and Heed's early encounter with Celestial, a woman who recognizes true empowerment and distances herself from the "counterfeit world" of Cosey's boat, where "women could dominate" (111). Understanding the terms of this domination, she keeps her distance. Celestial exemplifies *"the beauty of meaning much by saying little"*: Christine and Heed encounter her only once, but this contact has a profound effect. Playing on the beach, they hear a man call "Hey, Celestial"; a woman turns around and, seeing the two girls, recognizes with a wink the possibility of authentic empowerment in friendship. The phrase "Hey, Celestial" becomes part of the girls' discourse, used "to say 'Amen,' or acknowledge a particularly bold, smart, risky thing" (188). The novel ends with Celestial's lament for Cosey.

DISCUSSION QUESTIONS

- "Hard to know people. All you can go by is what they do" (43). By what means do we "know" the characters in *Love*?

- Each chapter of the novel is named for the different roles played by Cosey. Why does Morrison name the final chapter of the book "Phantom?"
- Morrison has used the image of a crystal to describe the structure of *Love*.[3] Why might she use this image?

11

TODAY'S ISSUES IN TONI
MORRISON'S WORK

Although Morrison sets many of her narrative lines in the past, contemporary themes pervade her work. Her novels testify to the endurance of tensions between personal and social conceptions of power, success, and fulfillment. These tensions manifest themselves in very different ways owing to historical determinants but nevertheless persist into the future. Speaking to Don Swaim in 1987, Morrison accepted his categorization of *Beloved* as a historical novel but stressed that some of its issues remain highly relevant for contemporary mothers seeking a balance between the demands of maternity and of the self. In *Paradise*, Morrison transports the reader back to 1976 but in writing the novel she aimed to "suggest something about negotiation that is applicable for the 1990s." She told Carolyn C. Denard that some of the tensions threatening to destabilize Ruby are in evidence today: "There are a lot of neo-cons, a lot of activists, a lot of pacifists, people for integration, people against integration, who are still out there."[1] The overarching concern of the "love" trilogy is particularly pertinent to the contemporary reader: "the problem of trying to love oneself and another human being at the same time is a serious later-twentieth-century problem, a very serious problem."[2]

Morrison has used her social criticism and her fiction to explore why this dilemma has particular currency in today's America. She has suggested that the discourses of the media and popular culture fuel the tension between autonomy and contingency, working against the individual's desire for self-knowledge and the search for authentic relationships. In interviews given over the past three decades, Morrison has repeatedly voiced her concern over the paucity of plots and models available to young people living in today's America.

She has noted that contemporary conceptions of fulfillment for many Americans depend entirely upon participation in one of the nation's most revered institutions: the nuclear family. In *The American Child: A Cultural Studies Reader* (2003), Caroline Levander and Carol Singley observe that "[n]arratives of U.S. national identity are persistently configured in the language of family."[3] As a writer who has explored intergenerational relationships throughout her fiction, Morrison is often asked to share her thoughts on America's continuing preoccupation with this institution. While she recognizes the necessity of familial love in novels such as *The Bluest Eye, Beloved*, and *Jazz*, she has expressed strong reservations about the kinds of ideals and expectations that have accumulated around the model of the nuclear family.

In 1989, Bonnie Angelo identified the rise of the single-parent family in American society as a cause for concern and asked Morrison to share her thoughts on the matter. Morrison immediately questioned hegemonic conceptions of "family": in particular, she queried the patriarchal bias underpinning today's pervasive anxiety about single mothers, asking why society continues to position the father as the head of the family. Morrison argued that the problem lies not in the distinction between one- or two-parent families; rather, all children require the nurturing of the community at large. Morrison is disheartened not by the rise in single-parent families but by the absence of this communal sensibility in modern America. She told Angelo that the obsession with the "nuclear family ... isolates people" and questioned America's elevation of this model above all other kinds of community. In today's social landscape, she sees a need for a "larger unit."[4] Three years after this interview, Morrison gave further expression to some of these thoughts in her novel *Jazz*. Dorcas's aunt, Alice Manfred, reflects at the age of fifty-eight on her own parents' obsessive fear that she would become pregnant as a young, unmarried woman. Acknowledging the absence of children in her life, Alice queries the need for the "hysteria, the violence, the damnation of pregnancy without marriageability" and recalls how quickly this sense of dread metamorphosed into anticipation on the day of her wedding (*Jazz*, 76).

One of Morrison's aims as an artist is to engage the reader's "willingness to see the other side of things."[5] In some of her novels, the roles and relationships associated with the nuclear family are revealed as potential sources of restriction and immobilization. Morrison has expressed admiration for *Sula*'s Hannah Peace who, unlike Nel's mother, does not try to control her children's development; her approach to mothering is, according to Morrison, "genuinely maternal." Deprived of other narratives through which to realize new conceptions of the self, members of nuclear families such as the Deads in *Song of Solomon* and the Streets in *Tar Baby* find themselves locked into roles, their language and behavior conditioned by hegemonic images of home and family. Outraged by her baby son's "implicit and explicit demand for her best and constant self," Margaret Street finds teaching him to walk both "a horror and a pleasure" (*Tar Baby*, 238). She can engage positively with her son only when he becomes an adult and their relationship can develop beyond the confines of received notions of familial identities. Narrating in the 1990s, *Love*'s L comments on the skewed vision of those parents who, intoxicated by the thought of becoming indispensable to another human being, are unable to comprehend other forms of love: mistaking "*dependence for reverence*," they cannot "*imagine anything more majestic to the child than their own selves*" and miss the joy experienced by their sons and daughters when they feel love for other children (*Love*, 199). In *Song of Solomon*, Macon Dead II views his position at the head of a nuclear family as confirmation of his upward mobility, yet as he approaches his house he sees its female inhabitants as stranded, defeated figures: in his vision of his wife, Ruth is reduced to her "narrow unyielding back" and his daughters are "boiled dry from years of yearning" (*Song of Solomon*, 28). The impact of Macon's arrival testifies to the pull of dominant conceptions of "family" on the Dead women; locked into their roles as wife or daughter, they rely on the presence of the patriarch to shore up their identities. Ruth Dead is one of Morrison's loneliest characters; for her, the identities of wife and mother have lost their currency. She seeks verification of an interior self not in her relationships with her husband and children, but in arbitrary yet familiar signs such as the water mark on the table: it becomes for her a kind of anchor, affirming the presence of a world beyond her home where she might one day engage the latent stirrings of an independent mind and spirit. Interaction within the Dead nuclear family is restricted to formulaic gestures and discourses. Macon Dead II recognizes that his house has none of the music of Pilate's home yet can communicate with his son Milkman only through imperatives or condemnations.

Through her fiction Morrison has shown that one does not need to belong to a nuclear family to fulfill the roles and possibilities associated with it. In her novels, some of the most intimate and enduring connections are forged outside the parameters of the nuclear family through identifications similar to the one experienced by Morrison when she encountered the fisherwoman.[6] The rich potential of such identifications finds expression in Shadrack's "always"; Nel's "girl, girl, girlgirlgirl," a realization that her friendship with Sula has informed her life more than her marriage to Jude (*Sula*, 174); Celestial's wink, a recognition of the power of Heed and Christine's friendship; the gaze of the washerwoman which teaches Valerian "limitlessness" (*Tar Baby*, 141); the "barefoot walk" with Reverend Misner which takes Deacon Morgan beyond the strictures of guarded exchanges with Ruby's men (*Paradise*, 300); Consolata and Dovey's dialogues with "strangers" who reflect back facets of their buried selves and the "loud dreaming" of the Convent women (*Paradise*, 264). Such connections empower characters to counter the gaze of the "sociological microscope[]" and the accompanying pressure to conform to social conventions.[7] This process is often activated by contact with a particular kind of character who resurfaces throughout Morrison's work. In an interview for O magazine, she told Pam Houston of her abiding preoccupation with the "anarchic figure" who, although rejected by the community, can bring other people to vital realizations.[8] The words and gestures of these figures are freighted with a deep understanding that resonates powerfully with keen watchers and listeners. Apprehending the "*beauty of meaning much by saying little*," Shadrack needs only one word to communicate a realm of possibilities to Sula, who remembers that word on her deathbed (*Love*, 3).

Morrison's imaginative world offers many points of entry for these figures. However she has suggested that this openness is not reflected in today's America, where social boundaries are becoming ever more fixed. In 1981, she spoke to Thomas LeClair about society's growing intolerance of nonconformists who choose to live on the fringes of communities, their lives unfettered by social codes and expectations. As a result of this resistance, future generations are less likely to benefit from the enriching encounters experienced by characters in her novels. Morrison wonders if the contemporary preoccupation with "be[ing] 'right'" is to blame for this disregard.[9] Another reason might be contemporary society's elevation of one particular kind of connection. One year before speaking to LeClair, Morrison commented on the emergence of a troubling hierarchy which places romantic love over the many forms of connection which extend over her fiction: the communal relationships so valued in the past have been overshadowed by an obsession with the prospect of finding everlasting romantic love: a prospect which, like the model of the nuclear family, encourages people to think of relationships as small, contained units.[10]

Morrison has used her fiction to illuminate the dangers of investing in this narrative. By writing themselves into the romance plot, her characters risk alienation from their community and heritage. While Milkman Dead's engagement with his ancestors enables him to gain a sense of momentum, his lover Hagar remains trapped in a cyclical present. Morrison uses images of violence to capture the intensity of this kind of "passion" and the helplessness of its victims: it "knocked her down at night, and raised her up in the morning, for when she dragged herself off to bed, having spent another day without his presence, her heart beat like a gloved fist against her ribs" (*Song of Soloman*, 127). Although Pilate's less conventional family unit offers the music missing in her brother's house, it is ill-equipped to deal with Hagar's immobilization; the youngest member of this household also requires contact with a wider community to flourish.

In *Love*, L's opening commentary registers the impact of the contemporary elevation of romantic love on society's use of language. Narrating at the end of the century, L despairs at the exhibitionism of local women who are desperate to inscribe themselves into the romance plot. She chooses to hum in protest at "*how the century is turning out*" rather than engage the signature terminology of the 1990s. Fueled by narrow conceptions of romantic love and the attendant need for self-dramatization, the dominant discourse among the local women betrays a lack of imagination or thought and reveals only that "*all is known and nothing understood*" (*Love*, 4). In the talk at the restaurant where she works, L hears little evidence of "*help from the mind*" (*Love*, 5). When the romance plot fails, the women respond by writing themselves into another formulaic narrative, moving seamlessly from romantic heroine to victim to explain why they are "*tough instead of brave*" and why they rely on self-display to attract attention: they fall back on stories of "*dragon daddies and false-hearted men, or mean mamas and friends who did them wrong*" (*Love*, 4–5).

Indifference to deeper levels of understanding stretches across social boundaries. The third-person narrator in *Love* sees little hope for the young people living on the Settlement, the derelict region where Junior was born and raised. The voice identifies a potentially mobilizing force in the fund of unheard stories and forgotten traditions known only to the older citizens; however, this generation is rarely consulted and so the people of the Settlement remain estranged from the rest of society. Resistance to new kinds of knowledge resurfaces further on in the novel, when Romen's grandmother Vida reflects with sadness on the apathy of contemporary children who close their ears to the stories of their ancestors.

Capitalist ideology poses a further threat to the connections dramatized in Morrison's fiction. In 1981, she noted that communal concerns
such as the transmission of narratives and values to younger generations
have been subsumed by "the political thrust to share in the economy and
power of the country."[11] The tensions between these concerns form the
central focus of *Song of Solomon*. Unable to visualize a life founded
upon the acquisition of gold, Milkman is mobilized by the thrill of reverence for the people of his past. Speaking about *Song of Solomon* at a
dinner party for Oprah's Book Club, Morrison addressed one of the
more common criticisms of her work: that her characters take on mythical proportions and they are "not realistic" but "bigger than life." She
shared her response with Winfrey and her dinner guests: "I keep saying
no, no, no, life is big, they are as big as life ... we make life small. We
make it tiny and think it only is our incomes." *Paradise* provides a vivid
example of this kind of contraction in the form of Steward Morgan's
narrative. His obsession with accumulation results in the erosion of his
senses and the literal reduction of his land, sacrificed to the oil industry.
When Dovey thinks of her husband, it is only "in terms of what he had
lost": his "sense of taste" and "the trees that made [their ranch] so beautiful to behold" (*Paradise*, 82).

At the *Song of Solomon* dinner, Morrison told Winfrey and her
guests that she wants her books to enlighten the reader to the possibility
of leading "an enchanted life." In her fiction, this possibility unfolds
through an engagement with a "larger unit," whether it is the wider
community, one's ancestors, or the natural world. Morrison's fiction
abounds with possibilities for such enchantment. It is apprehended in
the singing of Pilate, Reba, and Hagar, to which Macon II momentarily
"surrender[s]" (*Song of Solomon*, 29); the sensation of the "sweet gum's
surface roots cradling [Milkman] like the rough but maternal hands of a
grandfather" (*Song of Solomon*, 279); the "star-packed sky" observed by
L, which "made you feel rich" whatever "your place in life or your state
of mind" or Claudia's imagining of the perfect Christmas day (*Love*,
105).

However, the loss of such anchors as history and community leave
today's young people exposed on a fruitless search for enchantment. In
Tar Baby, the only novel by Morrison with a contemporary setting,
Jadine actively seeks out an unanchored existence; New York delights
her precisely because it seems to answer to her desire for a contemporary
identity. However, throughout the novel, Jadine is haunted by the sense
that she is missing out on some form of enchantment. She rejects openings into the past and refuses to acknowledge Ondine's claim on her as a
daughter but finds herself floundering at the end of the novel, seeing

little inspiration in the narratives available to her: "Every corner was a possibility and a dead end. Work? At what? Marriage? Work and marriage? Where? Who?" (*Tar Baby*, 159). In attempting to map out a life for herself and Son in the city, she "demands clarity, precision, very specific solutions to open-ended problems" (*Tar Baby*, 269), the kinds of answers that Morrison's novels rarely yield.

Jadine sees only two avenues to success for Son in the city: enrolling at a New York university or setting up a business with Valerian's money. Morrison has noted that capitalist definitions of power and success are problematic for African Americans such as Son: "it's a serious problem for black Americans who envision success in certain ways and have difficulty manipulating power once it's in their hands. Because the definitions of success and the ways in which one acquires and therefore *holds* power are quite different in a *totally* capitalistic country."[12] Success for Morrison's characters takes many different forms but always involves the acquisition of knowledge about one's self and one's potential: one's ability to "*ride*" the air, rediscover love for a friend, engage with one's ancestors, reinvent a romantic relationship, or find healing through testimony. Morrison has suggested that it is the internalization of received notions of power that has led to the estrangement of the classes in today's America. Speaking about *Love*, she has presented the story of Heed and Christine's friendship as a correlative to the history of their communities: when the two young friends first encountered each other, their social status had no impact on their mutual affection; in their community, the doctor and the truck driver were neighbors. Morrison has stated that the possibility of social mobility is essential but has also noted that it diminishes opportunities for familiar contact between the classes.[13]

In 2003, Henry Louis Gates Jr. witnessed the impact of class polarizations when he interviewed African Americans living in four widely different parts of the country. Initially, the interviews were recorded for a television documentary entitled *America Beyond the Color Line*. The accompanying book, *America Behind the Color Line: Dialogues with African Americans*, followed in 2004. Invoking W. E. B. Du Bois's hugely influential declaration that the "problem of the twentieth century is the color-line," Gates examines the experiences of African Americans at the beginning of the twenty-first century. In the introduction to his book, Gates identifies the common preoccupation that emerged from dialogues across the country: "Everybody's a CEO. Everybody's talking about entrepreneurship, products, markets, and market share. It's all about getting the most out of people, empowering, creating wealth."[14] Visits to affluent suburban neighborhoods in Atlanta and the Robert Taylor Homes, a Chicago housing project designed to provide economical housing but now dominated by poverty, drugs, and violence, revealed that "the problem of the twenty-first century is the problem of the color line as color is fractured or compounded by class." At the end of his four-part documentary, Gates calls for "a renewed civil rights movement" which must, he asserts, be led by Wall Street. He expresses some skepticism about this prospect, observing that, "for some reason it's harder to mobilize around issues of class than it is issues of race and racism."[15]

For his documentary, Gates visited Los Angeles in order to explore the racial politics of Hollywood's film industry. In the television episode devoted to this journey, Gates interviewed black people working in the film industry. Reginald Hudlin, the director of two hugely successful films, *Boomerang* and *House Party*, told Gates that racism continues to have an impact on the reception of black films no matter how successful they are. In today's market, a hit black film is "an invisible success ... a tree that fell in the forest that no one heard." The "color line" that Morrison exposes in novels such as *The Bluest Eye, Jazz*, and *Tar Baby* remains very much in evidence in contemporary Hollywood. Speaking to black actresses, Gates found that the industry continues to cast lighter-skinned over darker-skinned actresses. When he addresses the issue of what he terms "one of Hollywood's darkest secrets: the color line within the race," he finds that "small variations in skin tone can make or break a black woman's career."[16]

In recent years, Morrison has spoken optimistically about some dimensions of life for African American women living in the twenty-first century. In her novels, she explores the impact of dominant mythologies of beauty perpetuated by the film and beauty industries. Asked by a member of the public in 2008 if she thinks that contemporary young black women are facing the same struggle with self-image as did Pecola, the young girl who longed for blue eyes, Morrison responds with emphatic optimism, remarking on the "confidence" she sees in twenty-first-century African American women.[17] However, some of the issues raised by *The Bluest Eye* remain the subject of debate in today's beauty and fashion industries. At the beginning of the novel, Claudia reflects on the tyranny of the white gaze that has designated "a blue-eyed, yellow-haired, pink-skinned doll" as the paradigm of beauty and the measure of one's value (14). In July 2008, Italian *Vogue* published its first "black issue" featuring only black models. The magazine printed four versions of the issue, each presenting a photograph of a different model on the cover. The issue included interviews with Spike Lee, Michelle Obama, and Edmonde Charles-Roux, a former editor of Paris *Vogue*. Charles-Roux resigned from *Vogue* in 1966 in response to a decision not to use a cover featuring a black model named Donyale Luna. According to *Time* magazine, the first run of the July 2008 issue sold out in the United States and the United Kingdom in seventy-two hours.[18] Thirty thousand extra copies were printed for American readers alone. The publication and success of the issue prompted many people to speak out against the prevalence of racism in the fashion industry. When asked to comment on this, British photographer Nick Wright responded: "The fashion industry and the advertising industry are steeped in racism. You just have to look at the number of black girls you see in adverts—virtually nil. Among the main fashion brands, they are completely underrepresented. It's shocking and atrocious."[19] Although the July issue of Italian *Vogue* used only black models for its covers, its advertisements betrayed the continuing dominance of white paradigms in the contemporary world of fashion. Some of those commentators who applauded *Vogue Italia* were quick to point out that almost all of the advertisements in the magazine featured white women exclusively.

Morrison is often asked to share her vision of America's future. In an essay entitled "A Slow Walk of Trees," she outlines the contrasting perspectives of her grandparents on the future of race relations in America. She describes the vision of her grandfather, John Solomon, who throughout his life was "convinced ... that there was no hope whatever for black people in this *country.*" Her grandmother Ardelia had a more optimistic outlook and "believed that all things could be improved by faith in Jesus and an effort of the will."[20] Writing in 1976, Morrison reflected that both viewpoints could be sustained. Her interviews and essays published toward the end of the twentieth century suggest that little had occurred to alter this reflection. While economic progress gives her some cause for optimism, she has continued to voice her deep concern about the persistent tensions fracturing American society and affecting black people in their daily lives. The racism pervading America manifests itself in the violent treatment of black men and changes in "race talk" which, she observes, "is forced to invent new, increasingly mindless [stereotypes]" as "American blacks occupy more and more groups no longer formed along racial lines."[21]

In *Song of Solomon*, Milkman listens uneasily to the barbershop men who make jokes about the inevitability of being arrested whenever a crime is committed; the tension in their laughter testifies to their shared awareness of their vulnerability. Speaking to Zia Jaffrey in 1998, Morrison recalled her hopes on the birth of one of her sons, thirty years earlier: "I thought they were not going to ever have the experiences that I had ... that level of hatred and contempt that my brothers and my sisters and myself were exposed to." She tells Jaffrey that her optimistic outlook was unfounded and that the fears she felt for her sons as they grew up remain immediate at the end of the twentieth century: "black boys became criminalized. So I was in constant dread for their lives, because they were targets everywhere. They still are."[22]

In an interview with Rachel Cooke of the *Guardian* in 2004, Morrison expressed her sense that the country was "going backwards" and revealed that she was deeply troubled by the prospect of the re-election of George W. Bush: "I can't tell you how frightening it is—to see the battle we thought we had already won ... we're fighting to vote again ... This is a major crisis. We're at the edge of a cliff." The result of the 2000 election had left her "[p]aralysed, aghast, seething." She expresses incredulity at the Bush administration's reaction to the attacks of September 11, 2001: nobody "acted like a grown-up." She predicted that a Bush victory in 2004 would elevate the sense of fear shared by many Americans.[23]

Four years later, Morrison talked optimistically of the possibility of growth for America after the election of Barack Obama. During the campaign for the Democratic candidacy, Morrison endorsed Obama in a letter that was published in the *New York Observer* on January 28, 2008. Commentators expressed some surprise at this move, owing to the media's framing of Morrison's opinions of the Clintons.[24] In the letter of endorsement to Obama, Morrison expressed her respect for his fellow candidate Hillary Clinton, praising her commitment and recognizing her "knowledge" and experience. She revealed that race and gender have little to do with her choice of candidate; rather, she looks at the candidate's "quality of mind." She described Obama's candidacy as an "opportunity for national evolution (even revolution)" which "will not come again soon." In her fiction and social criticism, Morrison has given voice to her concerns about the narrowing of discourses, narratives, and ideals in today's society; in Obama, she sees "keen intelligence, integrity, and a rare authenticity" and a "creative imagination which coupled with brilliance equals wisdom."[25] When asked to respond to the outcome of the 2008 election in a *Fora* interview, she agreed that Obama's victory is a "cultural signpost," adding: "This is courageous. This is really like a restoration of principles that we have taken for granted or lied about and denied ... for a long, long time."[26]

DISCUSSION QUESTIONS

• At the end of *Sula*, Nel observes that "places" have vanished and that people have retreated to "separate houses with separate televisions and separate telephones and less and less dropping by" (166). How does

Morrison dramatize the consequences of this kind of retreat in her representations of contemporary society?

- What constitutes success for the characters in Morrison's novels? How do their personal notions of success, power, and fulfillment differ from those dominant in today's society?
- How does Morrison dramatize the difference between knowing and understanding in her fiction?

12

POP CULTURE IN TONI
MORRISON'S WORK

In her essay "On the Backs of Blacks," Morrison observes how the discourses of American popular culture have colluded in the perpetuation of negative, stereotypical images of African Americans. The language and imagery of popular culture is "heavily engaged in race talk" which "renders blacks as noncitizens, already discredited outlaws." Popular culture "participates freely in [the] most enduring and efficient rite of passage into American culture: negative appraisals of the native-born black population."[1] Its grip on modern America is such that it manages to counter the reality of engagements between immigrants and African Americans.

The narrowing impact of popular culture is a prevalent concern in Morrison's fiction. Her novels dramatize its refusal to testify to the richness and diversity of the lives of African Americans in a number of ways: the fashion industry is blind to the beauty of the African woman in the yellow dress in *Tar Baby*; the film industry excludes young black girls in favor of Shirley Temple; and in *Love*, the racist depictions of the advertising world condition May's contempt for Heed's family. Morrison's novels illuminate the dangers of observing popular culture's elevation of "destructive idea[s]" such as romantic love and physical beauty (*The Bluest Eye*, 95). While Claudia in *The Bluest Eye* rejects emphatically those narratives from which she is excluded, other characters seek identification in them. When Pauline Breedlove visits the cinema, she is presented with the easy visual integration of black and white images on screen that "came together, making a magnificent whole" (*The Bluest Eye*, 95). Although this clearly belies her daily reality, Pauline internalizes the formulaic narratives played out on the screen, leaving no space for the development of an autonomous self. In *Song of Solomon*, Hagar seems to have the upper hand in her relationship with Milkman, initially dictating its pace and terms. However, an early conversation with Milkman betrays her absorption of the romantic script churned out by the movie industry. Milkman tells her: "You're like all women. Waiting for Prince Charming to come trotting down the street and pull up in front of your door ... Violins playing and 'courtesy of MGM' stamped on the horse's butt" (*Song of Solomon*, 97). Hagar's ready and unqualified agreement with Milkman's assessment makes for one of the novel's most disconcerting moments. She turns in desperation to the codifications of the advertising world to win back Milkman, believing that her life will gain coherence if she embodies the beauty industry's idea of physical perfection. Morrison illustrates the stranglehold of commercial rhetoric over Hagar by particularizing the brands of each item that she acquires and their accompanying advertising slogans: "She bought a Playtex garter belt, I. Miller No Color Hose, Fruit of the Loom panties, and two nylon slips—one white, one pink—one pair of Joyce Fancy Free and one of Con Brio ('Thank heaven for little Joyce heels')." Struggling to contain her body inside the zipper of her skirt, Hagar becomes "convinced that her whole life depended on whether or not those aluminum teeth would meet" (*Song of Solomon*, 311). In *Jazz*, Felice reflects that Dorcas enters into a relationship with a married older man in an attempt to write herself into the script of the "plotting and planning" adventuress (*Jazz*, 201): "Everything was like a picture show to her, and she was the one on the railroad track, or the one trapped in the sheik's tent when it caught on fire" (*Jazz*, 202). She rejects Joe, a man who embraces her without judgement, for Acton, who acts as movie director of her own life.

Those characters whose lives approximate or fit the paradigms of popular culture also find themselves locked out of enriching relationships or experiences. In *Tar Baby*, Margaret's arresting, conventional beauty conditions all of her relationships and disqualifies her from parental manifestations of love. In contrast, the beauty of the African woman in yellow reflects a coherent, autonomous self: while Margaret must shrink from the gaze of others, the woman in yellow dazzles with her authenticity: Jadine "gasp[s]" when she sees this "woman's woman—that mother/sister/she; that unphotographable beauty" (43). It is crucial that while Jadine is overwhelmed by the woman in yellow's self-possession, she immediately sees her in terms of connections: the woman is a "mother/sister/she."

The tropes and discourses of popular culture have little currency for those with a more coherent sense of identity. In *Jazz*, Felice learns ways of challenging dominant mythologies from two generations and is therefore disconcerted by the hackneyed scenarios that Dorcas invites her to reconstruct. For Dorcas, they offer openings into new and exciting identities, but they leave Felice with a sense of disembodiment: "Nothing like me. I saw myself as somebody I'd seen in a picture show or a magazine. Then it would work. If I pictured myself the way I am it seemed wrong" (*Jazz*, 209). In *Tar Baby*, the "[s]paces, mountains [and] savannas" in Son's "forehead and eyes" reveal to Jadine a sensibility untouched by the discourses and preoccupations of popular culture (*Tar Baby*, 159). When she reads fashion magazine copy to Son, she must decode terms such as "fast lane," designed to depict the world within its covers as one of glamour, variety, and advancement (*Tar Baby*, 116). Son is already wary of the written word, having been disturbed by the media's depiction of America and becoming "suspicious of all knowledge that he could not witness or feel in his bones" (168). He is troubled by the television screen's flattening out of individual identity: "the black people in whiteface playing black people in blackface unnerved him. Even their skin had changed through the marvel of color TV. A grey patina covered them all and they were happy. Really happy." He can detect no individuality in their "televised laughter" (217).

Given her strong resistance to "the mindlessness that seems to have joined the smog of California's movie world," it is perhaps unsurprising that only one of Morrison's novels has so far been translated onto the cinema screen.[2] Speaking to Michael Silverblatt in 1998, she suggested that literary poetics are incompatible with the medium of film: "you have a major void in a movie which is you don't have a reader, you have a viewer ... [a]s subtle as a movie can be, as careful and artful as it can be, in the final analysis it's blatant because you see it.... The things that I can create and hint at via the structure, via the choice of words, via the silences are not the kinds of things that would be successful in any movie."[3] Moreover, the predominantly linear structures of film and television narrative cannot reflect our comprehension of time; people continue to "experience life as the present moment, the anticipation of the future, and a lot of slices of the past."[4]

Morrison maintained her skepticism about this kind of translation when she was approached by Oprah Winfrey about a cinematic adaptation of *Beloved*. From the start, Morrison told Winfrey that she would not participate in the project and questioned its viability. On reading the novel, Winfrey had sensed immediately that it not only could but "should" be made into a film; fewer than twenty pages into *Beloved*, she found that she experienced its narrative as a series of visual scenes and saw herself in the role of Sethe.[5] Winfrey had experience acting; she received an Oscar nomination for her role as Sofia in Steven Spielberg's commercially successful but controversial adaptation of Alice Walker's best-selling novel *The Color Purple* (1985). She also played the lead role in a miniseries of Gloria Naylor's short-story cycle, *The Women of Brewster Place* (1989), directed by Donna Deitch.

Winfrey bought the rights to *Beloved* before it received the Pulitzer Prize in 1988. Her belief in the project never foundered but it was nine years before she found in Jonathan Demme a director who shared her vision. His adaptation of *Beloved* would be the most expensive film to date to dramatize black life. Morrison had no direct involvement in the making of the movie but offered some advice on a visit to the set. Three writers collaborated on the screenplay: Akosua Busia, Richard Lagravenese, and Adam Brooks. Speaking to Charlie Rose in 1998, Winfrey described her preparation for the film. She did not play Sethe as a nineteen-year-old woman but wanted to undergo as immediate an experience of slavery as possible. She went to an underground railroad where she was renamed and led into some woods and blindfolded by people playing the role of the slave masters. She found out how the nineteen-year-old Sethe must have felt running in the darkness from Sweet Home, completely alone and with no certainty of reaching her destination. She reflected on this experience until she began to "come apart."[6] During the making of the film, she kept memorabilia of slavery in her trailer, which reminded her that she wasn't taking part in the film for herself.

Winfrey found that in order to play Sethe, she had to achieve some distance from the novel that had moved her so powerfully. After visiting the set, Morrison sent one note to Demme: "Oprah Winfrey is emotional. Sethe is not."[7] In the book *Journey to Beloved*, Winfrey reveals that she was concerned that she had not done justice to Morrison's vision. She heeded Demme's advice to bear in mind the differences between the media of film and literature. Winfrey's love of Morrison's language was restricting her from entering fully into the role of Sethe. She was particularly enchanted by a line where Sethe speaks of her twenty-eight happy days at 124 before revealing the events of the twenty-ninth day. After hearing her deliver the line, Demme told her that her reading would work well for an audiobook narration but would not convince audiences if delivered from the mouth of Sethe herself. When he observed that Winfrey was being stymied by her response to the book, she realized that she had to make the transition from reader to actor. In the interview with Rose, Winfrey confirms that the "hardest lessons came from exactly what Toni Morrison feared in not being emotional."

Morrison's novels pose particular challenges to filmmakers working within an industry that favors narrative fixity and chafes at moral ambiguity and complexity. However, Winfrey was not the only reader to pick up on *Beloved*'s cinematic qualities. Three years before the film's release, critic Lynda Koolish delivered an innovative reading of the cinematic characteristics of *Beloved*. Morrison has spoken of the "journey" of writing *Beloved* as the "track[ing] of an image from picture to meaning to text."[8] As Koolish notes, the characters in the novel, having been robbed of their language, experience memory as vision: Sethe expresses wonder at the tenacity of the "thought picture[s]" that enter her mind and "float[]" outside it as independent entities (*Beloved*, 43); Beloved, in striving to communicate the traumas of the Middle Passage, asks "how can I say things that are pictures" (248). Morrison has suggested that film as a medium cannot generate the same level of agency from its viewers as the literary text solicits from its readers. Koolish sees parities between Morrison's narrative tactics and the established techniques of filmmakers, using cinematic terms to describe Morrison's navigation of the novel's narrative layers: the movement between narrative lines and perspectives is achieved through shifts from the "long-shot" to the "disconcerting close-up" and the use of "asynchronous sound," techniques that foster a close engagement between literary text/film and the reader/viewer.[9]

Koolish's cinematic reading was in some ways prophetic. Demme exploited some of those characteristics of *Beloved* that she had identified as cinematic, using the camera to engage a range of perspectives. In his film, the attack on Sethe by schoolteacher and his nephews is dramatized from Sethe's perspective in an attempt to breach the distance between her and the viewer. In fleeting, disorienting flashes of the attack, the camera swerves around chaotically to the aggressive sounds of barking dogs and shouting and the sight of the men leering over Sethe; interspersed with these brief scenes are shots of Sethe narrating to Paul D while baking bread, her hand movements becoming increasingly pronounced. When Paul D first arrives at the house, we view him and Sethe talking on the porch from inside the house through the focalization of the "ghost" standing by the front window. At one point, Demme obliterates the distance between the viewer and Beloved; when she begins to walk around 124, we assume her focalization, immediately experiencing her disorientation; as she moves tentatively forward, the camera shakes: for a moment, the viewer becomes Beloved trying to reach her sister Denver across the room.

Some critics praised Demme for capitalizing on the highly visual quality of the novel. In his article on the film, Richard Corliss of *Time* magazine describes Demme's technique as "painterly." Writing for the *New York Times*, Janet Maslin singles out Demme's visual ingenuity for particular praise: for her, the visual touches are the most compelling manifestation of Demme's close engagement with the novel's world. However, in her detailed essay review of the film, "Freak Shows, Spectacles, and Carnivals," Anissa Janine Wardi queries the compatibility of the cinematic medium with the visual quality of the novel. There is, Wardi asserts, "no representational analogue to Morrison's textual project."[10]

When she visited the set, Morrison found some confirmation of her theories about the incompatibility of the two media. While Koolish argues that Morrison's techniques in this novel are inherently cinematic, Morrison found that her feedback on the issue of "where to linger, where not to" was of no use at all, precisely because her vision was not "cinematic."[11] However, Demme strives to emulate Morrison's *approach* in the film. Her novels shun exposition and explanation, calling forth the reader's agency, inviting reflection on the characters' motivations and the plot's implications by offering tantalizing glimpses of partially rendered stories. For Winfrey, Demme's handling of the exit of Howard and Buglar at the beginning of the film typifies his restraint: "He eliminated exposition from a scene and it turns out to be one of the best scenes I've ever done. He cut the fat, leaving just the essence. Sethe's sons are gone! What's to come?"[12]

As a whole, the movie strikes an uneasy balance between melodrama and restraint. Many reviewers objected to the early scenes in which the ghost asserts its presence at 124. Hereboy, the dog, is thrown against a wall and loses an eye as the house shakes and mirrors shatter; the handling of the haunting recalled for some reviewers the gothic extravagance of early horror films. Demme observes the basic principle of the novel's formal organization, representing the interplay of the past and the present through overlapping images. As Sethe and Paul D lie sleeping, multiple images fade in and out of the screen, filtered through rippling water: Paul D and Sethe asleep in 124; the attack on Sethe; Paul D chained in the yard at Sweet Home with the bit in his mouth; a traumatized Halle repeating the word "loft" and covering himself in butter in the yard. However, some important focalizations are lost in Demme's film. Morrison presents Beloved's death in increments and from a range of viewpoints. At the beginning of the film, Paul D walks through the red light in 124 and we are presented with a glimpse of Sethe standing in a shed with two babies in her arms. The movie does not return to this scene until Paul D presents Sethe with the newspaper clipping. The reactions of Baby Suggs and Stamp Paid to Sethe's act are not explored.

Although the film runs a lengthy 172 minutes, some of the novel's narrative threads are edited or truncated. In the novel, Morrison places Paul D's story next to Sethe's, but in the film, Danny Glover's Paul D gives an abridged account of his eighteen years of wandering. Sixo's story remains largely untold; it is reduced to brief glimpses and references. Some of the film's more protracted excursions into the past focus on the preaching of Baby Suggs in the clearing. Indeed, Demme gives the last word to Baby Suggs: before a final shot of 124, we witness her preaching in the woods, repeating the words "love your heart" and "this is the prize," pressing home one of the novel's most important messages about the meaning of freedom. Richard Corliss asserts that the film's "conclusion holds more hope than the book's." In his illuminating reading of the movie, Marc C. Conner expresses disappointment at Demme's handling of Beloved's final scene—she "vanish[es] ... in a cheap comic 'poof'"—but sees the film's closing scene as a "bold interpretive choice": it is, he feels, in keeping with the film's overarching message that "the ancient properties and remarkable endurance of wise women" are the keys to "survival and restoration."[13]

Punctuating the final scene between Paul D and Denver is a subtle touch that evokes a glimmer of hope for race relations. As noted in the chapter on *Beloved*, Morrison depicts Sethe and Paul D walking along the pavement and stepping aside for four women who ignore them. Demme shifts this moment to the end of the film; Paul D watches Denver walk away and is pleased to see that she is greeted by a young man. The man leads Denver away from the pavement as a group of white men approaches. While most of them walk on, seeing through the young black couple who have made way, one man pauses and tips his hat to Denver. While racism is still so entrenched that most of the white men do not even notice Denver and her companion, there is a single gesture of recognition.

Some of the novel's most ambiguous, challenging scenes find no place in the film. The wariness of the community toward 124 and its inhabitants emerges clearly—neighbors drive by and peer warily at the house—but is attributed only to disapproval of Sethe's act. The film does not explore the community's suspicion of Baby Suggs's generosity—indeed, her final days of looking at color are not addressed—or the collective unease with Sethe's air of self-sufficiency. The choking of Sethe in the clearing, one of the more ambiguous scenes in the novel, is edited out. The impact of Beloved's advances on Paul D is easily missed: after he capitulates to her sexual demands, the lighting turns red as he repeats the words "red heart": without repeated reference to Morrison's image of the tobacco tin heart, the significance of this is lost. Stamp Paid's role is diminished, his revelations functioning primarily as plot devices. The movie does not register the complexity of his feelings toward Sethe: admiration tempered by the resentment and suspicion that prompt him to show Paul D the newspaper clipping. In the film, he hands over the clipping in response to Paul D's announcement that he is planning to start a family with Sethe; there is little sense of conflict in Stamp Paid's decision to disclose Sethe's secret. The viewer does not learn the story of Stamp Paid's wife Vashti. When Denver visits the Bodwins' house looking for work, the money jar does not make an appearance.

Demme's *Beloved* sharply divided critics. Many found much to praise in its fidelity to some of the novel's strategies and messages. Perhaps most important, some reviewers felt that the film called for a "readerly" approach, inviting the kind of participation from its viewers that Morrison requires from her readers. Will Joyner of the *New York Times* notes: "[The film] reinforces a literary way of looking at things, whereby allusion counts for more than action or illusion"; the movie aims "to appeal to serious readers and to seduce non-readers."[14] Others disagree. Wardi argues that the editing of the film compromises the agency of the viewer, delivering "spoonfed emotions of fear, wonder, and curiosity that do not merely disrupt our reading response, but severely limit its scope."[15]

Some criticism betrayed discomfort with the violation of cinematic narrative conventions. Some reviewers felt that Demme should have eschewed Morrison's narrative strategies altogether; they registered objections to the shifts in viewpoint and, assuming that every film must have a protagonist, expressed confusion over the identity of the main character. In "Oprah's Belabored Beloved," John C. Tibberts writes that while the film is "an astonishingly faithful rendering of Morrison's text," its makers "unnecessarily complicated the already fractured storyline with an overindulgent use of slow-motion effects, sudden flashbacks, a barrage of persistently recurring image motifs...."[16] Much of the criticism leveled at the film came from reviewers who were clearly unfamiliar with the novel. Some reviews were riddled with inaccuracies and misinterpretations.

The aspect of the film that has most divided critics and viewers is the depiction of Beloved herself. Many reviewers framed their criticism with the speculation that she is an impossible character to render on screen. Morrison herself has stated that "she must be someone that the reader invents," adding that "when you're in a movie situation, you have a face. It fixes it."[17] While Thandie Newton's performance drew much praise, some viewers and critics felt that the representation of Beloved moved the film dangerously close to the melodramatic framing that its makers had tried so hard to avoid. Critics who were unfamiliar with the novel or had misread it tried to define Beloved in absolute terms, complaining that her identity as Sethe's lost daughter was obvious from the start. More perceptive critics praised Demme for leaving the question open. Edward Guthmann of the *San Francisco Chronicle* wonders if she was "a living ghost, a trickster? Or just an imagined entity—a receptacle for the fears and wishes of Sethe and her family?"[18] Many critics of the novel and Demme's adaptation have suggested that the excursion into Beloved's consciousness, in which the voices of those murdered and abused during the Middle Passage struggle to be heard, defies effective dramatization on film; however, as Marc Conner has noted, the film gestures toward these untold stories through Beloved's reference to "the dark place" where she is "small," the recurring visual representations of water, through which some memories of the past are filtered, and Denver's final comment on Beloved: almost an exact replica of her words in the novel, it encourages the viewer to think about Beloved as the embodiment of a wider narrative of oppression. Paul D asks Denver if she believes that Beloved was her sister. Kimberly Elise's Denver replies: "At times. At other times, I think she was more."

Much of Beloved's characterization in the film is dependent upon visual and aural cues. The sights and sounds of the natural world play a prominent role in scenes involving Beloved, who seems to be in tune with its nuances. Indeed, the natural world plays the same kind of choral role in Demme's film as it plays in Morrison's fourth novel *Tar Baby*. Framing one intimate domestic scene is the shot of a bird of prey circling 124, perhaps gesturing toward a presence beyond the house, anticipating a revelation or arrival or enacting Sethe's circling of the story she has tried to suppress. When Beloved first emerges from the river, she is surrounded by a host of fluttering butterflies and her wheezing and gasping is accompanied by a cacophony of buzzing and chirping. When Sethe, Paul D, and Denver return from the carnival and discover her resting against the stump, she is covered in crawling ladybugs. Many praised this approach to her characterization, suggesting that Demme had dismantled the boundary between the natural and the supernatural. However, Wardi felt that the association between Beloved and the insects conveyed the message that she should be regarded as some kind of threat. Of Beloved's entrance Wardi writes: "There is nothing ... that reveals [her] humanity, a fact compounded by her juxtaposition with the carnival."[19]

In the past, Morrison has expressed frustration at the way that the publishing world and media have framed her as *the* black woman writer, making room for no more. Given the scarcity of positive, full representations of black life on the cinema screen, it is perhaps inevitable that the film *Beloved* would be regarded in Hollywood "as almost a test case of whether studios will continue to finance the handful of serious films each year on black themes."[20] Anticipation for the movie was fueled by a vigorous advertising campaign and discussion on *The Oprah Winfrey Show*; however, most American viewers stayed away from screenings of *Beloved*. According to Bernard Weintraub, the film was most popular in big cities such as New York and Detroit, where the "prime audience ... appeared to be older black women."[21] Commentators have speculated on the reason for this resistance, wondering if it can be attributed to wariness of the subject matter or a general reluctance to watch lengthy, serious films. Reginald Hudlin has stated that "the black audience won't see period black films, because for them, anything in the past is literally pain."[22] Comparisons were made with Steven Spielberg's *The Color Purple*, a movie that made millions of dollars worldwide, yet sparked controversy over what some critics deemed its stereotypical representations and its capitulation to sentimentality. However, Spielberg's film appealed to audiences across different cultures. Marc C. Conner notes that those involved in bringing *Beloved* and *The Color Purple* to the screen did so with different goals in mind from the start: with *Beloved*, the goal was to "present as complex, uncompromising, and challenging a portrayal of African American history and culture as possible." Some of the most vitriolic criticism aimed at the film of *The Color Purple* centered on its dramatization of black men. In his reading of Demme's *Beloved*, Conner singles out the film's handling of black masculinity for particular praise, asserting: "the film's treatment of black male sexuality represents a landmark in the history of African-American film."[23]

Morrison's response to the movie remains tempered by ambivalence. Indeed, when Robin F. Whitten of *Audiofile* interviewed her about her narration of her audiobooks, he reported that "Ms. Morrison felt a certain urgency to complete the unabridged version of *Beloved* because of the film release."[24] On viewing the film, some of her reservations were immediately quashed. She says of Winfrey's performance: "As soon as I saw her I smiled to myself because I did not think of the brand name. She looked like Sethe. She inhabited the role." After three viewings of the movie, she concluded that, in some ways, it had responded to her hopes for her own novel: "They did something I thought they never could: to make the film represent not the abstraction of slavery but the individuals, the domestic qualities and consequences of it."[25] Reviewing the film on its DVD release in 2004, some critics shared an optimistic outlook on its future. Margaret A. McGurk predicts that Demme's *Beloved* will be "studied, debated, and cherished decades from now when Americans look to film for insights on who we are and where we have been."[26]

DISCUSSION QUESTIONS

- Having watched Demme's reworking of *Beloved*, to what extent do you agree with Morrison's statement that "[a]s subtle as a movie can be, as careful and artful as it can be, in the final analysis it's blatant because you see it?"
- The depiction of Beloved divided critical opinion. Did the filmmakers capture her role as history or was she reduced to a kind of "spectacle"?
- Consider some of the words, images, stories, and viewpoints that do not appear in Demme's adaptation of *Beloved*. Why did he edit these out and how might their inclusion have affected responses to the film?

13

TONI MORRISON ON THE INTERNET

Readers of Toni Morrison's work will find a wealth of useful material on the Internet, where sites offer links to essays, articles, and speeches written by Morrison or give accounts of her life and achievements. Many interviews with Morrison have been published exclusively online, as well as many critical readings of her fiction.

Morrison's novels explore the construction and reception of history, the pull of the past, and its interaction with the present. The Internet offers access to a wide range of material chronicling eras and events in African American history, including those that have been dramatized in Morrison's fiction. Jessica McElrath's African-American History Blog at http://afroamhistory.about.com is a generous Web site; it provides links to a wealth of information on "major events and moments in African American history," including textual documentation of slavery, Reconstruction, the Great Migration, the civil rights movement, and the Harlem Renaissance.[1] The Underground Railroad pages detail the history of the term, describe the routes taken by escaped slaves, and provide a further link to the text of the Fugitive Slave Law; the Harlem Renaissance pages feature helpful links to writers and key figures of the period; and pages chronicling the civil rights movement offer visual documentation of some of the most significant moments in the movement, such as the Emmett Till Rally and the 1963 March on Washington. This Web site also offers a link to Tom Head's "Illustrated History of Civil Rights" and a "Civil Rights Timeline." Information on Morrison can be found at

McElrath's site under the "People" and "Writers" links; further links lead to a range of online resources on Morrison, including biographical accounts of her life, essays and interviews, the Nobel lecture, and a bibliography.

Highly informative online resources can be found at the Washington Library Web site at http://www.lib.washington.edu. This offers links to numerous sites focusing on particular eras in African American history under titles such as "Civil Rights," "Civil War and Slavery," "The African-American Migration Experience," and "Harlem History." There is a link to Dr. Gwendolyn Midlo Hall's database, "Afro-Louisiana History and Genealogy 1718–1820," where one can find original documentation detailing information about slaves and their testimonies. The site also provides access to thousands of slave narratives and links to biographies of African American writers, politicians, sociologists, and historians, including W. E. B. Du Bois and Frederick Douglass.

The Toni Morrison Society Web site (http://www.tonimorrisonsociety. org) is a useful reference point for readers interested in finding up-to-date news about Morrison and the scholarship associated with her work. The society was established in 1993 before Morrison was awarded the Nobel Prize. The Web site provides news about Morrison, photographs of society events, and a detailed bibliography of critical material on her work. One of the society's major events involved the "bench by the road" project that was inspired by an image from Morrison's acceptance speech for the Melcher Book Award, presented to her by the Unitarian Universalist Association in 1989 for *Beloved*. The speech, which is available at http://www.uuworld.org, draws attention to the absence of a location or space in which "to summon the presences of or recollect the absences of slaves." The Toni Morrison Society Web site provides photographs of a memorial ceremony held by Morrison and 300 others on Sullivan's Island, where a bench was placed to "honor[] the memory of enslaved Africans who arrived on Sullivan's Island and of those who died during the Middle Passage."[2] As well as offering a full transcript of Morrison's acceptance speech, the Unitarian Universalist Association Web site includes an illuminating question-and-answer session on *Beloved* with members of the award ceremony audience. Felicia R. Lee's report on the memorial service at Sullivan's Island can be found at the *New York Times* Web site, http://www.nytimes.com.

Numerous literature Web sites offer valuable information about Morrison, her fiction, and the work of writers who share some of her thematic concerns. The Voices from the Gaps site (http://voices.cla.umn. edu/vg) is a "Web-based transnational academic community" that provides resources on "the lives and works of North American minority women artists and writers."[3] The Web site's Toni Morrison page is a helpful starting point for readers of Morrison's fiction; it provides a biography, analysis of *The Bluest Eye, Sula,* and *Beloved,* and gives consideration to various critical responses to these novels. A bibliography of critical material and links to other Toni Morrison sites are also included. The site http://womenshistory.about.com features a useful page on Morrison written by Jone Johnson Lewis. As well as a biography, the site provides links to quotations, book summaries, a bibliography, the Nobel lecture, and Morrison's highly informative *Salon* interview with Zia Jaffrey. Random House's Web site, http://randomhouse.com, provides summaries of all of Morrison's novels and some of her nonfiction as well as links to biographies and excerpts from her audiobooks.

Anniina's Toni Morrison Page at http://www.luminarium.org/contemporary/tonimorrison/toni.htm is a particularly rich Web site and an excellent reference point for those readers seeking detailed explorations of Morrison's novels. This site contains links to individual pages dedicated to each of Morrison's novels, as well as bibliographies, interviews, and biographies. Pages focusing on specific novels offer further links to critical reviews and readings and related articles and interviews. The *Beloved* page features a link to an excerpt from Morrison's audiobook narration of the novel.

Further helpful material can be found at http://www.oprah.com, the Web site that accompanies Oprah Winfrey's television show and magazine, *O.* Pages on *The Bluest Eye, Sula, Song of Solomon,* and *Paradise,* all of which were selected for Oprah's Book Club, offer biographies of Morrison, plot synopses, and questions about the novels. Pages on *Sula* include illuminating excerpts from the transcript of the original book club discussion of Morrison's second novel. Winfrey, Morrison, and the invited readers discuss the representation of maternity in *Sula* and consider what the novel can tell us about the potential and the intricacies of female friendship. Oprah.com also features an article by Philip Weinstein entitled "Faulkner 101: Toni Morrison and William Faulkner." Weinstein recognizes Morrison's reservations about these kinds of comparative readings; he looks at work by both writers while remaining wary of the "pitfalls" of evaluating them in terms of how they "correct" or "measure up to" each other.[4]

The Oprah Web site also provides some very useful material on Morrison's eighth novel, *Love.* The link "Toni Morrison Talks Love" leads to "The Truest Eye," where Pam Houston shares details of her discussion with Morrison. The discussion is divided into three sections: "Love," "On Writing," and "The Greater Good." Morrison speaks to Houston about recurring dimensions of her work, such as the "idea" of "a wanton woman": "An outlaw figure who is disallowed in the community because of her imagination or activity or status" but whose "presence is constructive in the long run." Morrison cites Sula and Junior from *Love* as examples of this figure.[5]

A wide range of material on Morrison can be found at *Time* magazine's Web site. These pages contain numerous interviews, reviews of Morrison's work, and articles by and about Morrison. In a 1998 interview with Paul Gray, "Paradise Found," Morrison discusses her seventh novel, the impact of the Nobel Prize on her life, and the effects of Oprah's Book Club on her book sales. The interview concludes with Morrison's thoughts on the concept of paradise: "It's not my place to define paradise for anyone else…. But I'll confess what my idea of paradise would be for me. Nine days of seclusion, total seclusion. No obligations, no demands, nothing but doing anything I wanted, when I wanted."[6]

The *Time* magazine page "Nobel Prize-Winning Author Toni Morrison" has a transcript of an interview between Morrison and Timehost, again conducted in 1998, where Morrison answers questions submitted by readers online. When one teacher asks Morrison to recommend some learning activities for students studying *Beloved*, Morrison characteristically hands the agency over to the students and suggests that they write their own guide to the novel. Morrison also speaks about teachers who influenced her. This page features links to some of Morrison's essays such as "On the Backs of Blacks," "The Dancing Mind," and "The Pain of Being Black," the interview with Bonnie Angelo that focuses primarily on issues arising from *Beloved*. On another useful page from the *Time* Web site, "10 Questions for Toni Morrison," Andrea Sachs reads questions submitted by readers in 2008, ten years after the Timehost interview. Issues covered include Morrison's endorsement of Barack Obama and the representation of gender politics in *The Bluest Eye* and *Song of Solomon*. This interview is also available as a video. Richard Corliss's highly informative report on the filming of Jonathan Demme's *Beloved* for *Time* magazine is also available online and includes Morrison's thoughts on the filmmaking process. Many reviews of Demme's *Beloved* are available online, including those cited in the chapter on Morrison's engagement with popular culture.

The *New York Times* Web site provides links to a generous range of new and illuminating material on Morrison. "Toni Morrison's Mix of Tragedy, Domesticity, and Folklore" is an interview-article by Dinitia Smith covering aspects of Morrison's life and work with a particular focus on *Paradise*. The site also provides access to A. O. Scott's article "In Search of the Best," which details the search for the best work of American fiction of the last twenty-five years. The *New York Times* consulted "a couple of hundred prominent writers, critics, editors, and other literary sages" for their thoughts; *Beloved* received the most votes, finishing "solidly ahead of the rest." The article discusses the book's impact on American readers and its place in the American canon and provides a link to Margaret Atwood's review of the novel, "Jaunted by their Nightmares."[7] The *Times* Web site also features a Toni Morrison Web page with further links to various articles by and about the author: a piece by William Grimes on her receiving the Nobel Prize; an interview with Mervyn Rothstein about *Beloved*; reviews of *Margaret Garner*, the operetta for which Morrison wrote the libretto; and reviews of a theater production of Lydia Diamond's adaptation of *The Bluest Eye*.

Reviews, interviews, and articles published in the *Guardian* newspaper and Web site are available at http://www.guardian.co.uk. In the article "Ghosts of a Brutal Past," American novelist Jane Smiley examines the novel's legacy. There are also links to three reviews of *Love* and a review of *Paradise*. Maya Jaggi's profile of Morrison provides some useful insights from the author and can also be found at the *Guardian* Web site.

Another interview can be found at http://www.salon.com/books/int/1998/02/cov_si_02int.html. In February 1998, Zia Jaffrey asked Morrison about issues arising from *Paradise*. Morrison shares her thoughts on the critical reception of the novel and its representation of gender politics. She reveals that of all the male characters in *Paradise*, she identifies most with Richard Misner. In this interview, she also speaks about her writing process, revealing that it continues after the book is published; she will return to her novels years later and think about what she might have edited or expanded upon. Regarding *Paradise*, she tells Jaffrey that she would have liked to include "another kind of confrontation with Patricia, the one who kept the genealogies together."[8] Morrison also reveals whether or not she thinks that writing can be taught and speaks about her relationship with her editors.

A highly informative, thirty-minute interview with Don Swaim, conducted for CBS Radio in 1987, is available on the Wired for Books Web site. One can hear Morrison talking about her childhood, her work as an editor for Random House, the conception of *Beloved*, and her thoughts on its contemporary relevance. The Wired for Books Readers' Comments: Toni Morrison page at http://wiredforbooks.org/morrison.htm offers links to the Swaim interview and to a lively discussion of *The Bluest Eye* between two professors and a scholar of literature from Ohio University.

Some television interviews with Morrison are now available on the Internet. Her extensive interviews with Charlie Rose can be viewed online. Interviews conducted in 1993, 1998, and 2003 are available on Google Videoplay. In the 2003 interview, Morrison discusses and reads from *Love*. The 1998 and 2003 interviews are also available on the Charlie Rose Web site, as is Rose's interview with Morrison, Jessye Norman, Clarissa Pinkila Estes, and Judith Weir, who, along with Maya Angelou, collaborated on woman.life.song. In this interview, Morrison speaks about the differences between writing lyrics and novels: she describes the particular challenge posed by lyric writing as "stunning": "one works hard as a novelist to have it all—the music, the space, the silence, the narrative. But when you're writing lyrics, somebody is going to do that, somebody's going to put the music there so you, you say it, but you take it down, you take it down a level."[9] The Charlie Rose Web site also provides Rose's interview with Oprah Winfrey on the cinematic adaptation of *Beloved*. Other useful exchanges available online include an interview for amazon.com with James Marcus entitled "This Side of Paradise," in which Morrison answers questions about her seventh novel, and a 2003 radio conversation with Tavis Smiley for NPR that focuses on the publication and reception of *Love*. A further interview with *Audiofile*'s Robin Whitten focuses on the publication of Morrison's novels as audiobooks; Morrison speaks warmly about the level of interaction generated by this method of transmission.

In an interview for CBS, available on http://cbsnews.com, Morrison speaks about the experience of writing children's literature with her son Slade and reflects on the different ways in which maternal love manifests itself across the generations: "What my grandmother thought was love of her children was really staying alive for them. What my mother thought was love of her children was to get a better place, maybe enough money to send you to college if you wanted to. What I thought was love of my children was giving them the maximum amount of freedom, setting an example of how you could make choices in your life."[10] Information on the conception and reception of Morrison's children's writing can be found at the Connect for Kids Web site (http://www.connectforkids.org). The page entitled "Toni Morrison's Challenge" includes an interview with her conducted by Rob Capriccioso. Here she speaks about her son Slade's response to Aesop's fables; his observations were followed by a dialogue between mother and son, which formed the basis of the series of children's books *Who's Got Game?* Capriccioso asks Morrison to comment on the reception of her children's books, noting that some parents have raised objections against their depictions of adult/child relationships with their emphasis on the need to respect the agency and autonomy of the child. In response, Morrison reveals that she has encountered manifestations of the parental conduct represented in the books: teaching at various universities, she has met students who have been so conditioned by their parents' sensibilities that "their only job is to win." When asked to comment on parental responses to her second children's book, *The Book of Mean People*, she refers immediately to the enthusiasm of the intended audience: the children she has spoken to "*love*" the books.[11]

The Internet offers a wealth of critical material on Morrison's fiction. Some of the most illuminating articles on her novels can be found at http://www.findarticles.com. Anissa Janine Wardi's article on the depiction of Beloved in Demme's film can be found here, as can a highly informative, seventeen-page interview with Carolyn Denard conducted for *Studies in the Literary Imagination* entitled "Blacks, Modernism, and the American South: An Interview with Toni Morrison." Morrison discusses her own and her ancestors' experiences of the South and her depiction of Southern history in her novels from *The Bluest Eye* to *Paradise*.

DISCUSSION QUESTIONS

• Look at the sites on African American history noted in this chapter. How might these sites inform readings of Morrison's work?
• Look at the range of online interviews with Morrison. How useful are they to readers of her novels? In what ways might particular comments by Morrison or the interviewers change one's approach or reaction to her fiction?
• What can one learn about Morrison by looking at the different Web sites that are dedicated to her life and work? Do any recurring themes emerge? What aspects of her life and work most interest her readers? Is there any difference between the general public's reception of Morrison's work and the response of the media?

14

TONI MORRISON AND THE MEDIA

In her Nobel lecture, Morrison identified the "faux-language of mindless media" as one example of the way in which language is used to stymie and obstruct open dialogue.[1] She has returned to this subject repeatedly in her fiction, essays, and interviews, exposing the ever-diminishing range of perspectives that the media, in its ever-proliferating incarnations, chooses to engage. Such was Morrison's concern about the narrowing effects of the media's representations in the summer of 1998 that she formed strategies to evade its images and discourses. One story had dominated the news since the beginning of the year: President Bill Clinton's affair with Monica Lewinsky. Having lost faith in reporters to do little more than speculate and sensationalize, Morrison opted to rely on more traditional methods of gleaning news. She would draw from "conversation, public eavesdropping, and word of mouth."[2]

Concern about the totalizing instincts of the media has of course found expression in Morrison's fiction, particularly in *The Bluest Eye*, *Song of Solomon*, and *Tar Baby*. Her most extensive examination of the media's pernicious influence on modern America can be found in her nonfiction, where she has scrutinized the representation of black people in the public eye. In 1993, Morrison introduced and edited *Race-ing Justice, En-gendering Power: Essays on Anita Hill, Clarence Thomas, and the Construction of Social Reality*, a collection of scholarly essays examining the media's handling of the Clarence Thomas hearings in 1991. After the retirement of Supreme Court Justice Thurgood Marshall,

President George H. W. Bush nominated Clarence Thomas, a conservative black Republican. Thomas's confirmation was placed in doubt when law professor Anita Hill came forward with charges of sexual harassment against him. In her introductory essay to *Race-ing Justice*, "Friday on the Potomac," Morrison gives a brief account of these events but notes that the issues arising from them defy neat recapitulation. The media, with its contracted scope and gaze, could not possibly begin to engage with the complexity of the questions that emerged from the case. The essays in *Race-ing Justice* aim to scrutinize its ramifications by exploring issues that the media chose either to ignore or to distort; each exploration provides a much-needed corrective to the skewed coverage offered by the media. Morrison and her fellow contributors adopt the same approach to the case as she takes to her fiction, directing the reader's attention toward the distortions and gaps in official accounts and encouraging reflection on a range of perspectives.

As the nomination process unfolded, the media deployed a range of strategies to distort and sensationalize the story. Morrison's analysis of these strategies and their effects reveals deep concern about the enormity of the media's cross-cultural influence on modern America and its policing of public opinion. She notes that people of different races, classes, genders, and creeds consulted the media for confirmation of their responses, but that its coverage reduced the story to reassuringly succinct "bits and bites." Television screens appeared to promise interaction through regulated call-in spots which masqueraded as outlets for honest debate; engagement with viewers was conditioned by the agendas of the news anchors: callers who added "flavor [and] reinforcement" were welcomed, as were those whose "routine dissent" enabled news stations to flaunt their impartiality.[3]

Morrison writes that the hearings themselves became "an exchange of racial tropes": while Thomas was "cloaked in the garments of loyalty, guardianship, and ... limitless love," Hill "was dressed in the oppositional costume of madness, anarchic sexuality, and explosive verbal violence." Morrison draws attention to one of the most telling gaps in the Clarence Thomas case: the absence of exploration of his response to Hill's accusations. Denying the charges, Thomas could only attribute them to resentment of his choice of a white bride. The media showed little interest in Thomas's reaction, choosing instead to draw from stereotypical codifications of black female identity to represent Hill: "she could be called any number or pair of discrediting terms and the contradictions would never be called into question, because, as a black woman, she was contradiction itself, irrationality in the flesh."[4]

In her Nobel lecture, Morrison recalls Abraham Lincoln's words on the limitations of language in the Gettysburg Address: "The world will little note nor long remember what we say here. But it will never forget what they did here." Morrison responds: "his simple words are exhilarating in their life-sustaining properties because they refused to encapsulate the reality of 600,000 dead men in a cataclysmic race war. Refusing to monumentalize, disdaining the 'final word,' the precise 'summing up,' acknowledging their 'poor power to add or detract,' his words signal deference to the uncapturability of the life it mourns ... [l]anguage can never 'pin down' slavery, genocide, war. Nor should it yearn for the arrogance to be able to do so."[5] Morrison asserts that the media uses language in just such a way, to close down inquiry and establish totalizing narratives and images; it can be relied upon only to thwart the public's desire for new perspectives and to designate the shelf life of a story.

In "Friday on the Potomac," Morrison closes her analysis of the Clarence Thomas/Anita Hill case on a note of optimism, turning to the full and rich dialogue taking place beyond the media's glare as a result of the case: "In matters of race and gender, it is now possible and necessary, as it seemed never to have been before, to speak about these matters without the barriers, the silences, the embarrassing gaps in discourse. It is clear to the most reductionist intellect that black people think differently from one another."[6]

Four years later, Morrison examined the media's influence on public perception in her analysis of its handling of the O. J. Simpson case. She co-edited a volume of scholarly essays entitled *Birth of a Nation'hood: Gaze, Script, and Spectacle in the O. J. Simpson Case*. Her introduction scrutinizes the shaping of the "definitive" story of the Simpson case, arguing that it exemplifies the media's grip on public opinion in late-twentieth-century America. The definitive story took shape through "blasts of media messages" driven by the media's exploitation of the case's marketability. Simpson was the perfect "commodity," not only because of his achievements and talent, but also because of his race: "When race culpability or pathology is added to this market brew, profits soar and the narrative coalesces quickly, takes on another form, and moves from commodity to lore. In short, to an official story."[7] This surge toward the "official story" stifled impulses toward impartiality; any lines of inquiry that might have undermined or shed new light on the official story were foreclosed. Accounts of Simpson's life were riddled with gaps: in particular, Morrison notes, the media showed no interest in Simpson's life with his black family.

Morrison has witnessed the limiting effect of the media's language in the creation of her own public persona. She has remained wary of "media madness," sensing that if she were to "become [her] name in caps," she would risk the loss of the authentic "feelings and perceptions" that underpin her fiction.[8] In conversation with Charlie Rose in 2003, Morrison spoke of "keep[ing] out" the public persona of "Toni Morrison" and asserted that this construction has no bearing on the reality of her own life.[9] In particular, she has rejected those labels deployed by the press and the publishing world that ignore her history and heritage: she is troubled when she is viewed in terms of her credentials as an American or a female novelist; she has "insisted ... upon being called a black woman novelist" in recognition of the "access" she has had "to a range of emotions and perceptions that were available to people who were neither."[10]

Morrison speaks openly about her interest in the critical reception of her fiction. She told Zia Jaffrey that while some authors cut themselves off from this reception, she does not believe in this kind of isolation.[11] Reviews do not affect the way that she writes or regards her own work. Rather, it is her concern with the reception of African American literature, in particular that which is written by women, that motivates her to read reviews of her fiction. The reviews that fail to earn Morrison's respect are those that reduce the complexity of her work by viewing it within the parameters of a limited gaze. Such reductions are, she has noted, particularly prevalent in reviews of black literature. Speaking to Charlie Rose, she recalled a review of *Sula* that warned Morrison that she would "have to face up to the real responsibilities and get mature and write about the real confrontation for black people, which is white people, as though our lives have no meaning and no depth without the white gaze."[12] Particularly offensive are those reviews that treat books by African American writers as "sociological revelations." One reviewer compared representations of the black family in *Beloved* and *The Cosby Show* and another drew comparisons between a novel by Morrison and those of two other black writers, even though there was no resemblance between their writing strategies. The review concluded by picking the "best" of the three works, the only criterion being the proximity of their characters to "'real' black people."[13] When Thomas LeClair observed that black and white critics have claimed that Morrison presents "eccentric" characters who "aren't representative," Morrison responded: "This kind of sociological judgment is pervasive and pernicious. 'Novel A is better than B or C because A is more like most black people really are.' Unforgivable. I am enchanted, personally, with people who are extraordinary because in them I can find what is applicable to the ordinary."[14] She also finds the hierarchical mentality of some reviewers unhelpful: when a review described *Love* as a "return to Nobel-worthy form," Morrison responded: "it's a way of ranking your novels ... the way they do commercials of baseball games. It's totally unlike what writers think, I suspect, about their work."[15]

In recent interviews, Morrison has expressed optimism about the reception of black literature and stated that reviews have greatly improved. Regarding her own work, *The Bluest Eye* was largely disregarded or misunderstood, while *Song of Solomon* garnered almost universal praise. *Beloved* and *Jazz* remain her most popular books among reviewers. Responses to her later works often refer the reader back to these novels as the finest examples of Morrison's artistic achievement. While *Beloved* is remembered primarily for its visceral effect on the reader, *Jazz* is often singled out for its dazzling style and skillful manipulation of form. Although it was generally well received, *Paradise* provoked some negative responses from reviewers who took exception to what they perceived to be a more didactic strain in the novel and appealed for a return to the openness of *Jazz*. Morrison has been asked several times to comment on a particularly harsh review of *Paradise* by *New York Times* book critic Michiko Kakutani, who showed no recognition of the nuances of the novel, dismissing it as a "heavy-handed, schematic piece of writing."[16] In the 1998 interview with Rose, Morrison compared this response to an eleventh-grade book report, noting that Kakutani had relied on a facile plot summary to sustain her criticism. In the same interview, Morrison said that she welcomed those reviews of *Paradise* that steered the reader away from easy categorizations; she pointed to Paul Gray's response in *Time* magazine that noted the limitations of reading *Paradise* as a feminist novel. She also spoke with some humor about the level of conviction with which reviewers identified "the white girl" in *Paradise*.[17]

Morrison's social commentary also has provoked strong reactions from the media, in particular her questioning of America's preoccupation with the paradigm of the nuclear family. In a 1989 interview with Bonnie Angelo for *Time* magazine, Morrison was asked to comment on the rising number of young, unmarried mothers in America. Morrison queried the motivation for this concern over the maternal credentials of teenage mothers, noting that the grandparents of these mothers had children during their adolescence. She suggested that this widespread concern is inflected by race and class prejudice; commentators seem to experience or give voice to their disapproval only when the young mothers are black or come from impoverished backgrounds. Angelo, clearly surprised by Morrison's response, observed that young women living toward the end of the twentieth century in America have more access to education than their ancestors and should be encouraged to become doctors or teachers before taking on the role of mother. Morrison argued that motherhood is not the obstacle standing in these women's way: rather, it is a question of economics. Society does not want to have to pay for the education of teenage mothers. Morrison was promptly ridiculed for these views by some sectors of the American press. *The New Republic* magazine accused her of painting an idealized picture of teenage motherhood and characterized her "message" as "hostile to progress for American blacks."[18] This response typifies the media's misinterpretation and misappropriation of Morrison's social commentary; when she speaks out, she is viewed as a spokeswoman for all African Americans.

Further distortion of Morrison's words occurred when her article decrying the media's handling of the Monica Lewinsky scandal—the story that had dominated the news and which Morrison had tried to avoid—was published in *The New Yorker*. In "The Talk of the Town," Morrison referred to President Clinton as "our first black president."[19] Of all of Morrison's comments, it is perhaps this one that has aroused the most controversy among the media and the American public. Sectors of the media took this identification as their cue to take a closer look at Clinton's racial politics. Morrison's comment continues to find its way into interviews. In a Timehost interview conducted in 1998, she responded to a member of the public's appeal for clarification by asserting that her remark was taken out of context and misinterpreted. She explained that she was referring specifically to the *media's treatment* of Clinton during the Monica Lewinsky scandal, not offering an evaluation on Clinton's racial politics: "I was deploring the way in which President Clinton was being treated, vis-à-vis the sex scandal that was surrounding him. I said he was being treated like a black on the street, already guilty, already a perp. I have no idea what his real instincts are, in terms of race."[20] She also has attributed the original observation to comedian Chris Rock.

In a 1998 interview with Paul Gray for *Time* magazine, Morrison shared some of her thoughts on the media, revealing that she rarely watches television because it does not offer her a true reflection of the world: "I think of [television] as one of those false fireplaces, always moving and always looking the same." She spoke about forthcoming promotional appearances for *Paradise* with trepidation, expressing particular unease with the rigid schedules of television's morning shows: "'I just can't handle those two-to-five-minute snippets. I'm not good at it, and I sort of don't think much of the people who are good at it."[21]

In interviews with various figures from the media, Morrison is quick to point out the perniciousness or irrelevance of a particular question. When one interviewer resorted to asking her if she typed or wrote out her prose by hand, she responded: "You've really collapsed now, haven't you?"[22] She often draws a firm line between issues pertaining to her personal and professional lives. She feigned dozing off when Charlie Rose prepared to ask her about her personal life. When he asked her in 1993 if she was religious, she replied in the affirmative before asking: "You don't want to go any further than that, do you?"[23]

Not all forms of media have proved hostile to Morrison's desire for full, open, and honest dialogue. Since winning the Nobel Prize, she has made an increasing number of appearances on radio and television, using the media as a platform to reach people who might not otherwise read one of her books and to engage further with established readers. Critics are beginning to examine Morrison's engagement with the entertainment media in some detail, taking particular interest in her appearances on the phenomenally successful television program *The Oprah Winfrey Show*. For six years, Oprah's Book Club was one of the show's most successful features. Each month, Winfrey recommended a contemporary novel to her audience of millions and invited authors and readers to the show to discuss its themes and representations. Over the six years, four of Morrison's novels were selected for discussion: *Song of Solomon, Paradise, The Bluest Eye*, and *Sula*, respectively. When asked to justify the selection of a fourth Morrison novel, Winfrey asserted Morrison's centrality to the book club project: "for all those who asked the question 'Toni Morrison again?' with my fourth selection of her work, I say with certainty there would have been no Oprah's Book Club if this woman had chosen not to share her love of words with the world."[24] The show featuring *Song of Solomon* took the format of a discussion over dinner at Winfrey's home between Morrison, Winfrey, and a few selected readers. When *Paradise* was selected, viewers were invited to write a letter describing how the novel had affected them; those whose letters were chosen were given the opportunity to attend a seminar with Morrison and Winfrey.

Morrison initially regarded Winfrey's project with skepticism, questioning the extent of Winfrey's influence over the public's choice of reading matter. Her skepticism was checked when sales of her novels featured on the show rocketed after her appearances. Owing to "The Oprah Effect," a phrase coined by *Publishers Weekly* to reflect the phenomenal impact of Oprah's Book Club, *Song of Solomon* reached the best-seller list for the first time, twenty years after its publication. It maintained this position for sixteen weeks. Morrison has since described Oprah's Book Club as a "reading revolution."[25] In an article in the *New York Times Magazine*, "The Oprah Effect," D. T. Max reports that an average of 13 million viewers tuned in to watch shows devoted to the book club, 10,000 wrote requests to participate in the show, and 500,000 had made their way through at least part of the selected novel by the time the show aired; almost the same number would purchase the selected book after watching the show. Oprah's Book Club catapulted twenty-eight books to best-seller status and, it is estimated, made $175 million for publishers.[26]

Just as Morrison challenges categorizations based on race, class, and gender, she also chafes at some of the classifications fostered by the publishing world. Throughout her career, she has aimed to do away with the notion that a popular work of literature does not test the reader on an intellectual level: "I would like my work to do two things: be as demanding and sophisticated as I want it to be, and at the same time be accessible in a sort of emotional way to lots of people, like jazz."[27] The forum of Oprah's Book Club helped Morrison to challenge preconceptions about popular forms of literature. Cecilia Konchar Farr, a professor of English and women's studies, wrote a highly illuminating study of the book club and its cultural impact. In *Reading Oprah: How Oprah's Book Club Changed the Way America Reads*, Farr explores the reasoning behind Winfrey's selections and the order in which she presented them to America. She delivers analyses of some of the book club shows, focusing particularly on those featuring Morrison, who made more appearances than any other author. Farr demonstrates the centrality of Morrison's role in shaping the book club and enabling Winfrey to bridge the gap between conceptions of the popular and the literary. She notes that many of the selected books explored personal and social issues that had arisen repeatedly on Oprah's shows. Winfrey herself has noted parities between the subjects of several of her shows and the themes of *Song of Solomon*, her second selection for the book club. However, Winfrey also recognized that Morrison's novels, more than anyone else's, would enable her to share the benefits of close and precise reading and to encourage readers to return to the book in question and develop their own interpretations. In the shows featuring Morrison, readers repeatedly express a desire to reread the novel in question; those who appeal to Morrison for explanations of particular representations or events—a common theme is an appeal for the definitive version of a contested or partially rendered narrative—are usually advised to reread the novel. During the *Paradise* seminar, Winfrey's friend Gayle King asked Morrison to verify Billie Delia's interpretation of events in Ruby; Morrison replied: "If it's worth writing, it's worth going back to."[28]

It is this emphasis on active reading and engagement with the text that distinguishes Morrison's appearances on Oprah's Book Club from the promotional press events that she has found so limiting. In the essay "Toni Morrison, Oprah Winfrey, and Postmodern Popular Audiences," John Young argues that Morrison's engagement with Winfrey's audience counters easy dismissals of popular culture and undermines concerns expressed by other writers about possible conflicts between art and commercialism: "It is … vital to recognize that Morrison's interaction with Oprah produces more than just another example of contemporary society's obsession with media events, as the actual experience of reading *Song of Solomon, Paradise*, or *The Bluest Eye* intersects with these texts' transformations into objects of TV discourse. In the end, Winfrey and Morrison both emphasize the experience of reading these books, not simply consuming them."[29] In her novels, Morrison refuses to offer fixed meanings through the assertions of an obtrusive narrative voice; in her engagement with the book club audience, she refuses to close down inquiry with definitive interpretations of her novels. When Winfrey shares her confusion over the epigraph of *Paradise*—she tells Morrison that she "didn't get it"—Morrison responds that she does not "believe" Winfrey and that she must have approached it "with some heightened expectation." She tells Winfrey that if she read it to her again, she would immediately know what it signified.[30]

The success of Oprah's Book Club prompted debate in the publishing world about the public persona of the contemporary writer of literature. When his celebrated novel *The Corrections* was selected, Jonathan Franzen chafed at the association with some of Winfrey's choices that he deemed sentimental. He has since voiced his regret to *The Oregonian* over the way that his response was interpreted, attributing his resistance to concerns about commercializing his novels.[31] For Young, the contrasting responses of Franzen and Morrison to Winfrey's project raise interesting questions about the impact of race and gender ideology on the image of the literary writer. While white males actively cultivate the persona of the "isolated genius," black women writers need to "attain public identities in order to be recognized as authors."[32] Indeed, Morrison has never demonstrated any interest in the hallowed status of the novelist as sequestered genius. In her 1981 keynote address to the American Writers Congress, she declared: "Elitism rests its case on the conviction that that which is rare is better than that which is plentiful. Elitists do not consider the possibility that that which is rare may simply be scarce (like smallpox), not better." She highlights the dangers of the romantic concept of the isolated artist and calls for its banishment and for the implementation of "a heroic writers' movement" in its place.[33]

Young notes that publishers' interest in black literature has always been conditioned by the white gaze: if white people express a sporadic interest in black writing, a market is secure. Writing in 2001, he observed that there has been a shift away from this "racialized hierarchy," a shift that he identifies with the success of Oprah's Book Club.[34] Winfrey's success as a talk show host has long been attributed to her ability to engage audiences across cultural boundaries. As commentators such as Young and Timothy Aubry have noted, it is this cross-cultural appeal that made her show such a fertile site for discussion of Morrison's work, which encourages readers to think beyond racial and social identifications.

DISCUSSION QUESTIONS

- By what means does Morrison depict the narrowing impact of the media's language in her fiction? You might begin by looking at *The Bluest Eye, Song of Solomon,* and *Tar Baby.*
- Many reviews of Morrison's novels are available on the Internet and are cited in the bibliography. Read some of them and analyze their use of language. Do reviewers tend to focus on particular aspects of her work? How helpful are these reviews to Morrison's readers?
- Morrison has expressed astonishment at the impact of Oprah's Book Club on sales of her work. Why did Winfrey's shows prove such an effective medium for Morrison in reaching new readers?

15

WHAT DO I READ NEXT?

When invited to comment on connections with other writers of fiction, Morrison has often responded with caution. She has expressed reservations about the kinds of comparisons that have been drawn between her novels and those that have evolved from a different tradition. The writers whose works are cited here come from a range of traditions and have been chosen because their fiction shares thematic concerns with Morrison's or because they have a similar vision of the exchange between writer and reader.

In 2008, Morrison's ninth novel was published. *A Mercy* transports the reader further back than her previous novels, to the seventeenth century. Speaking to Lynn Neary, Morrison explains that she aimed to examine a time when "what we now call America was fluid, ad hoc" and when "owning the labor of people was a constant in the world so that was not the unusual thing. The unusual thing was coupling it with racism, which came much, much later." In writing *A Mercy*, she aimed to "separate race from slavery."[1] Page numbers cited from *A Mercy* are from the 2008 hardback edition (London: Chatto).

In *A Mercy*, Morrison again solicits the agency of the reader by developing narrative lines in increments and withholding elaboration of the most pivotal moments. In the opening sections, we learn that a slave woman gave away her young daughter, Florens, to an Anglo-Dutch tradesman named Jacob Vaark. It is not until the end of the novel that we hear from Florens's mother who, in a narration addressed to her daughter, explains that giving her away was "a mercy." The novel is composed of a series of interwoven stories concerning Florens and the people who live and work on Jacob's farm, all of whom are dispossessed in some way. The action unfolds through a series of third-person focalizations and the first-person accounts of Florens and, in the final section, Florens's mother. Jacob's English wife Rebekka is the daughter of religious fanatics. She comes to America to begin the "career[]" of wife, which, of the limited options available to women, seems to offer the most security.[2] Rebekka gives birth to four children, but they all die. She strikes up a friendship with the servant Lina, a Native American woman whose tribe was wiped out by smallpox. The most isolated girl on the farm is named Sorrow; her tenuous sense of identity springs from dim memories of "the only home she knew," the ship captained by her father (115). She is taken in by a family but rejected when she gets pregnant by one of the sons and is passed on to Jacob. At the farm, she takes solace in conversations with an imaginary "Twin" until she gives birth to a baby. Empowered by the "legitimacy" of motherhood, she changes her name to "Complete" (131). Florens's story unfolds across six sections that frame the stories of Rebekka, Jacob, Lina, Sorrow, and Scully, an indentured servant on the farm. Her first-person narration is addressed specifically to the man for whom she has developed an all-consuming passion: a free African who has worked on the farm as a blacksmith.

Through the narration of "love-disabled" Florens, Morrison dramatizes the dangers of surrendering one's sense of identity to sexual passion and romantic love (42). The most self-defining characters in *A Mercy* have a strong sense of heritage. While sweeping Jacob's floor, Lina "decide[s] to fortify herself by piecing together scraps of what her mother had taught her before dying in agony" (46). The blacksmith sees the approval of his ancestors in the owls that arrive to "bless" him as he works (66). Looming over the novel is the threat of further dispossession: after the death of Jacob Lina reflects that, should Rebekka die, the "unmastered women" will be "subject to purchase, hire, assault, abduction, exile" (56).

The blacksmith, whose name is never revealed, has healing powers and saves various inhabitants of the farm from smallpox. When Rebekka falls ill, Florens is sent to find him; her narration covers the length of her journey. When she finds her lover, he returns to the farm to help Rebekka but rejects Florens, telling her that she must learn to "own [her]self" (139). Unable to extricate herself from the either/or sensibility of a woman consumed by passion, she attacks the blacksmith and leaves him, unaware of his fate.

Many of the perpetrators of the horrific abuse in the novel attempt to justify their actions in the name of religion. As in *Paradise*, Morrison opens up questions about biblical representations, particularly in relation to gender ideology. Rebekka wonders what kind of "complaint a female Job would dare put forth?" and reflects that a female incarnation of Job "would have known and heard every minute of her life" the lesson that "shocked [him] into humility and renewed fidelity" (89). She senses that the feeling of displacement following the loss of her husband has and always will be the fate of women, destined to follow in the footsteps of Eve, "the first outlaw" (96).

Love and *Paradise* end with empowering moments of unity between women who have broken out of roles forged primarily through their relationships with men. At the end of *A Mercy*, Scully wonders about the "consequences of women in thrall to men or pointedly without them" (154). He reflects that the women on the farm have generated a "false" sense of community. While he "s[ees] nothing yet on the horizon to unite them," he also recalls the curate's representation of "what existed before Creation ... dark matter out there, thick, unknowable, aching to be made into a world" (154).

As Morrison noted in her interview with Lynn Neary, the dilemma facing this community of women remains central to American life: how to develop an autonomous identity without sacrificing one's relational sensibility.

When asked to identify writers who have influenced her, Morrison has spoken of crucial encounters with several African writers, including Chinua Achebe, Bessie Head, and Camara Laye, who "could assure the centrality of their race because they were Africans" and "didn't explain anything to white people." Her encounter with Achebe's novel *Things Fall Apart*, was pivotal: "[It] was more important to me than anything only because there was a language, there was a posture, there were the parameters. I could step in now and I didn't have to be consumed by or concerned by the white gaze. That was the liberation for me."[3]

Things Fall Apart (1958) is set in the Nigerian village of Ibo in the late nineteenth century. The novel dramatizes the impact of British colonialism on Africa's rich and varied culture. It centers on a man named Okonkwo, a highly respected farmer and the champion wrestler of the village, who defies European rule and fights against the erosion of his culture. As Simon Gikandi notes, the novel explores "the relationship ... between Okonkwo's individual crisis—of authority and power—and the crisis of his community, which increasingly finds its defining characteristics (including notions of wealth, marriage, worship, language, and history) undermined and transplanted by the new colonial order."[4] Achebe does not idealize Africa's past and invites the reader to ask questions about African culture. Okonkwo's son Nwoye silently queries the gender politics of his village when he reflects that, in order to observe the village's patriarchal ideology, he must suppress his preference for the stories told by his female relatives.

Laye's novel *The Radiance of the King* (1954) also informed Morrison's cultivation of a particular language and narrative method. In her review of the novel, she praises Laye for "summon[ing] a sophisticated, wholly African imagistic vocabulary in which to launch a discursive negotiation with the West" and choosing to "invite" rather than "tell" the reader to reconsider his or her preconceptions of Africa.[5]

When Gloria Naylor suggested to Morrison in 1985 that she was "the first widely accepted black woman writer," Morrison reminded her of the work of two predecessors: Zora Neale Hurston and Paule Marshall.[6] Hurston, whose work Morrison read after she had written *Song of Solomon*, was one of the writers of the Harlem Renaissance. She wrote a range of novels, short stories, and anthropological studies. Her books include a volume of folktales and songs entitled *Mules and Men* (1935) and her most celebrated novel, *Their Eyes Were Watching God* (1937). Set in Eatonville, Florida, *Their Eyes* charts the journey of its heroine Janie toward self-determination. Like Morrison, Hurston dramatizes the importance of telling and listening for personal growth. In his groundbreaking analysis of *Their Eyes Were Watching God*, Henry Louis Gates Jr. identifies the novel as a "speakerly text": one "whose rhetorical strategy is designed to represent an oral literary tradition." Janie narrates her story to her friend Pheoby who, like many of the listeners in Morrison's fiction, facilitates the telling. Gates notes: "Who speaks, indeed, proves to be of crucial import to Janie's quest for freedom, but who sees and hears at all points in the text remains fundamental as well. Pheoby's 'hungry listening,' we recall, 'helped Janie tell her story.'"[7]

Paule Marshall's novel *Brown Girl, Brownstones* was published in 1959. It tells the story of Selina Boyce, a Caribbean American girl living in an African American community in Brooklyn. The novel explores two searches for identity: "As [the heroine] struggles to find herself, the community is desperately trying to differentiate themselves from this new environment to keep their culture alive."[8] Like Morrison, Marshall emphasizes her debt to her community and her ancestors for her language and narrative method: those writers whose literature she admires are "preceded ... by another set of giants ... the group of women around the table long ago." Her work springs from "the rich legacy of language and culture they so freely passed on to me in the wordshop of the kitchen."[9]

Asked about the "direction" of black women's fiction, Morrison emphasizes the "incredible range" of work by writers such as Marshall, Alice Walker, Maya Angelou, Jamaica Kincaid, and Toni Cade Bambara.[10]

Morrison and Alice Walker are the most commercially successful African American women writers of their generation. When asked what drives her to tell particular stories, Walker often points to Morrison's motivation for writing: "It has been said that someone asked Toni Morrison why she writes the kind of books she writes, and that she replied: because they are the kind of books I want to read. This remains my favorite reply to that kind of question. As if anyone reading the magnificent, mysterious *Sula* or the grim, poetic *The Bluest Eye* would require more of a reason for their existence than for the brooding, haunting *Wuthering Heights*, or the melancholy, triumphant *Jane Eyre*."[11] Several critics have explored thematic resonances between Walker's most celebrated novel, *The Color Purple* (1982), and Morrison's first novel, *The Bluest Eye*: both explore the search for a language and sense of identity unconditioned by the white gaze and examine the impact of white ideology on black family life. However, Morrison and Walker approach these themes in very different ways. As several critics have noted, *The Bluest Eye* registers the impact of historical and social contexts to a greater extent than *The Color Purple*.[12] By the end of Morrison's novel, Pecola retreats into her imagination and has no means of communicating with the world; Walker's Celie finds a voice and language with which to assert her self-realization. Critics have also explored parities between the eponymous heroines of both writers' second novels: Morrison's Sula and Walker's Meridian are women who refuse to surrender their autonomy and are consequently treated as "outlaws." Both novels explore the ramifications of the heroines' self-definition on familial and romantic relationships.

Morrison has expressed much admiration for the African American writer Toni Cade Bambara. Morrison edited Bambara's work, including her final novel, *Those Bones Are Not My Child* (1999), which was published four years after Bambara's death. The novel explores the issues arising from the murders of more than forty African American children in Atlanta in 1979 and 1980. Morrison has described Bambara as a "reader's writer" and her writing as "woven, aware of its music, its overlapping waves of scenic action." Describing the experience of editing Bambara's fiction, Morrison writes: "In some manuscripts traps are laid as the reader is sandbagged into focusing on the author's superior gifts or knowledge rather than the intimate, reader-personalized world fiction can summon"; Bambara's fiction features no such traps, leaving space for the reader to work.[13] Like Morrison, Bambara believed firmly that all art is political. Her first novel, *The Salt-Eaters* (1980), is set in the small town of Claybourne, Georgia, and follows the recovery of disillusioned civil rights activist Velma Henry after her attempted suicide. It centers on Velma's relationship with faith healers Minnie Ransom and

Old Wife but also explores the experiences of other patients whose conditions stem from concerns about social and political issues in the wider world. Morrison also collected Bambara's essays, short stories, and interviews in *Deep Sightings and Rescue Missions: Fiction: Essays and Conversations* (1996).

To date, Gloria Naylor has written five works of fiction, all connected by recurring characters, themes, or settings. Although generally categorized as novels, three of these works are short-story cycles: *The Women of Brewster Place* (1982), *Bailey's Café* (1992), and *The Men of Brewster Place* (1998). All five of Naylor's works explore issues of race and gender and dramatize the pull of place and community on the self. During their published conversation, Naylor and Morrison discuss the differences between male and female discourses and relationships. In both Brewster cycles, Naylor explores the different ways in which men and women build friendships and communities. Naylor uses the story cycle form to point to the possibility of connection—themes recur and characters echo each other—while dramatizing the issues that isolate people from each other. Some of Brewster's women experience problems with self-displacement similar to those faced by Morrison's female characters. Describing the immobilization of Etta Mae Johnson, the narrator tells us that, "she was existing as she always had. Even if someone had bothered to stop and tell her that the universe had expanded for her, just an inch, she wouldn't have known how to shine alone."[14] *Bailey's Café* presents a more open, fluid community, placing stories by men and women side by side. References to jazz and blues frame the stories, pointing to the possibility of transcending social boundaries.

Maya Angelou's celebrated work *I Know Why the Caged Bird Sings* (1970) is the first of a series of autobiographies chronicling her personal journey through various social and cultural contexts. The book takes the reader back to Angelou's childhood in 1930s Arkansas and documents her early encounters with racism. Angelou's account of her struggle against the white gaze resonates strongly with Morrison's depiction of Pecola in *The Bluest Eye*. The fourth volume in the series, *The Heart of a Woman* (1981), records Angelou's experience of the Harlem Renaissance, her involvement in the civil rights movement, and her work with Dr. Martin Luther King Jr.

Morrison has described Jamaica Kincaid's work as "incisive and beautiful at the same time."[15] Kincaid shares some thematic concerns with Morrison, exploring the intricacies of familial relationships and the tensions between individual and communal identity. She drew from her own life for *Annie John* (1985), a series of linked stories charting the development of a girl growing up in Antigua in the 1950s. As she strives to assert her independence, Annie must come to terms with her contradictory feelings toward her mother and with the island's history of colonial oppression. She attends a school that is run by British teachers who ignore the island's history and frown on any engagement with its native culture. It is through contact with her female relatives that Annie learns about this culture; as a spiritual healer, Annie's grandmother is the only person who can save her granddaughter from a long and serious illness. Although Annie leaves the island in the final story, her mother tells her: "It doesn't matter what you do or where you go, I'll always be your mother and this will always be your home" (147).[16]

Morrison's engagement with the conventions of the slave narrative has been the subject of several critical readings of her work. In "The Site of Memory," she discusses texts such as Frederick Douglass's *Narrative of the Life of Frederick Douglass, an American Slave, Written by Himself* (1845) and Harriet Jacobs's *Incidents in the Life of a Slave Girl, Written by Herself* (1861).

In his narrative, Douglass reveals how he endured "the hell of slavery," exposing its devastating impact on his sense of identity.[17] In the opening of his narrative, he tells us that he was severed from his mother and can only guess at his age and speculate on the identity of his father, whom he believes to be a slave owner. In detailing his survival, Douglass registers the power of literacy to shape one's conception of one's self. Douglass eventually escapes to the North but leaves out several details of his escape narrative in order to protect the identities of those involved in helping him secure his freedom. Harriet Jacobs's *Incidents in the Life of a Slave Girl* gives expression to some of the ways in which women were affected by slavery. She recounts to the reader some of the most traumatic losses, such as forced separation from her children. In order to escape her abuser and oppressor, Dr. Flint, she lives for almost seven years in a tiny garret in the roof of her grandmother's shed. She escapes to the North but by the end of the narrative has yet to be reunited with her children.

Postmodern incarnations of the slave narrative genre include Sherley Anne Williams's novel *Dessa Rose* (1986) that was inspired by the lives of two historical women. Odessa Rose was a pregnant black woman who was involved in a protest by slaves on their way to a market to be sold. She was captured and sentenced to be hung but was given a reprieve until her baby was born. Ruth Elizabeth (named Rufel in the novel) was a white woman who lived on a remote farm in North Carolina and gave shelter to escaped slaves. The women never encountered each other in real life, but they meet in Williams's novel and forge a friendship that challenges the associations that have become attached to the figures of the slave woman and the white mistress.

Like *Beloved*, Gayl Jones's novel *Corregidora* (1975) dramatizes the recovery of buried stories and gives expression to the complex workings of memory. Jones sent the manuscript of *Corregidora* to Morrison, who recognized it as a literary landmark: "What was uppermost in my mind while I read her manuscript was that no novel about any black woman could ever be the same after this." Jones's prose offered Morrison a "reading experience" that "creates delight" and "strips away editorial expertise and goes straight to the jugular."[18] Like Morrison, Jones draws from oral and musical traditions, presenting her stories without projecting her own reactions or thoughts onto the page. The novel is narrated by blues singer Ursa Corregidora, who must articulate through song the experiences of abuse and oppression suffered by her maternal ancestors at the hands of a Brazilian plantation owner, Corregidora. The novel was well received, although some reviewers and readers have expressed reservations about Jones's frank treatment of sexual oppression.

Ralph Ellison's highly acclaimed novel *Invisible Man* (1952) dramatizes the impact of the white gaze on an African American man. Readers and critics have drawn comparisons with Morrison's treatment of this theme, focusing particularly on broad resonances between Ellison's novel and Morrison's *Song of Solomon*. However, there are clear differences between their approaches. Ellison's novel charts an African American man's struggle for self-definition in a world that is controlled by the white gaze. The hero-narrator retreats from the world and lives in a hole where he begins to record his story. While Morrison's Milkman Dead finds a sense of identity in his heritage, Ellison's invisible man finds no space beyond the white gaze. Unlike Morrison's Milkman, the hero of *Invisible Man* capitulates to Western notions of fulfillment: he "disdains the authentic Black folk history that has partially formed him" and "readily accepts the version of success projected by the dominant culture."[19] Morrison has queried the novel's exclusion of other gazes— "*Invisible Man* begs the question, invisible to whom? Not to me"—and has suggested that gender identity plays a significant role in shaping responses to the white gaze. Speaking about her own experience as a writer, she reveals: "It was amazing how freed up the canvas became once I took white people out as predominant figures. The only people who did that were black women: black men write about white men because they're their nemesis."[20]

Morrison recognized her debt to writer James Baldwin in a tribute written shortly after his death in 1987 for the *New York Times Book Review*. Here she expresses her gratitude to Baldwin for his "gift": a "language to dwell in." She writes: "No one possessed or inhabited language for me the way you did. You made American English honest—

genuinely international."[21] The intertextual relationship between Morrison and Baldwin has been the subject of much critical study. Comparisons have focused on the writers' treatment of race and gender politics and their engagement with the aesthetics of jazz and blues. Baldwin's novel *If Beale Street Could Talk* (1974) is an exploration of various incarnations of love that refuses conventional narrative closure. Moving between the past and the present, the novel tells the story of Fonny and Tish, a young couple living in Harlem in the 1970s. When Fonny is falsely imprisoned by a racist legal system, the community must battle to secure his freedom. As Joyce Carol Oates observes, the novel "affirms not only love between a man and a woman but love of a type that is dealt with only rarely in contemporary fiction—that between members of a family."[22]

Critics continue to make comparisons between the work of Morrison and William Faulkner, focusing on shared formal and narrative poetics and thematic concerns. Faulkner's novels examine relationships between the generations and races in America's Deep South and explore the pull of history, place, community, and nature on the individual. Many of his works take place in the fictional location of Yoknapatawpha County, Mississippi. Like Morrison, Faulkner invites the reader to query totalizing accounts of the South's history by repeating stories and rendering them from a range of perspectives; he rejects the limitations of linear structures and enacts through his forms the paradoxical workings of memory. Critical comparisons of Faulkner and Morrison often center on their treatment of racial issues. Faulkner has been both praised and criticized for his representation of black people in his novels. When asked how she has responded to stereotypical depictions of African Americans in his work and other "classics of American literature," Morrison has replied: "I skipped that part. Read over it. Because I love those books." She adds: "As for Faulkner, I read him with enormous pleasure. He seemed to me the only writer who took black people seriously. Which is not to say he was or was not a bigot."[23] Faulkner's most celebrated works include *The Sound and the Fury* (1929), *As I Lay Dying* (1930), and *Absalom, Absalom!* (1936). *Go Down, Moses* (1942) has been categorized both as a novel and a short-story cycle. Seven interlocking stories rendered from a range of perspectives challenge official accounts of history by dramatizing the impact of racism in the post-Civil War South.

Another Southern writer for whom Morrison has expressed admiration is novelist and short-story writer Eudora Welty. Like Faulkner, Welty has received both praise and criticism for her representations of black people. Morrison has stated that she "write[s] about black people in a way that few white men have ever been able to write. It's not patronizing, not romanticizing—it's the way they should be written about."[24] Writing about her relationship with her reader, Welty emphasizes the importance of connection rather than consensus. When asked to explain her engagement of her characters' experiences and sensibilities, Morrison has compared her method to that of an "actress": she speaks of "her willingness to bear witness and to view the world from her or his point of view." She adds: "I'm not judging and I'm not condemning and I'm not twisting them."[25] Introducing her *Collected Stories*, Welty describes a similar process: "I have been told, both in approval and accusation, that I seem to love all my characters. What I do in writing of any character is to try to enter into the mind, heart and skin of a human being who is not myself. Whether this happens to be a man or woman, old or young, with skin black or white, the primary challenge lies in making the jump itself."[26] Although her novels are widely celebrated, Welty is perhaps best known for her short stories. *The Collected Stories of Eudora Welty* includes her favorite and arguably most celebrated work, the story cycle *The Golden Apples* (1949). The cycle takes place primarily in a fictional town called Morgana in the Deep South and features several "outlaw" characters who live on the fringes of the community and who perform a similar function to the "anarchic figure[s]" who appear in Morrison's fictional world.

Many contemporary writers use variations on the cycle form to explore the relationship between the individual and the community. Most of Louise Erdrich's texts form a kind of macrocosmic cycle chronicling the lives of Native Americans from connected communities. Erdrich draws from the oral traditions of her Native American heritage, placing stories from a range of tellers side by side and repeating them with variations to stress their provisional nature. The best starting point for Erdrich is her first story cycle, *Love Medicine* (1987), recognized by Morrison on its release for its "beauty" and "power."[27]

Maxine Hong Kingston's work challenges definitions of the "real," defies generic categorization, and testifies to the value of the oral tradition. *The Woman Warrior: Memoirs of a Girlhood Among Ghosts* (1976) is a cycle of stories composed of fragments of memories, folktales, and historical and autobiographical accounts. The text's five stories are narrated by the Chinese American narrator-heroine who draws inspiration from the narratives she has learned from her relatives. Like many of Morrison's characters, Kingston's narrator finds that by telling stories, she is able to arrive at a more coherent sense of self.

Morrison has often spoken of her love of Latin American literature, in particular that of Colombian writer and fellow recipient of the Nobel

Prize, Gabriel García Márquez. Like Morrison, Márquez invites the reader to engage history's suppressed stories. He has identified his "most important problem" as "destroying the lines of demarcation that separate what seems real from what seems fantastic": although he has been situated within the relatively modern category of magical realism, he traces this vision back to his grandmother, who "told things that sounded supernatural and fantastic ... with complete naturalness."[28] Márquez himself achieves this effect in *One Hundred Years of Solitude* (1967). Like Faulkner, he created his own mythical town as a setting for his novel; Macondo is founded by José Arcadio Buendía and nineteen other families. The novel explores the impact of historical conditioning on an apparently self-defining community, following a century of civil wars, love affairs, and generational conflicts.

NOTES

CHAPTER 1

1. Morrison, "Charlie Rose: November 21, 2003."
2. Morrison, *Playing in the Dark*, 15, my italics.
3. Stepto, 10.
4. Dreifus, 101.
5. Morrison, "Audio."
6. Morrison, "Charlie Rose: May 7."
7. Jaffrey, 151, 152.
8. Koenen, 78.
9. See Koenen, 78–9, for Morrison's observations on this link between her personal experience and her fictional world.
10. Morrison, "The Fisherwoman," 142.
11. Dreifus, 100.
12. Gates, *Loose Canons*, 92.
13. Morrison, "A Bench" in Denard, *Toni Morrison*, 46.
14. Morrison, "An Hour."
15. Morrison, "Afterword," *The Bluest Eye*, 172.
16. Morrison, "A Bench," in Denard, *Toni Morrison*, 47.
17. Gates, *Loose Canons*, 143.
18. Morrison, "A Bench," in Denard, *Toni Morrison*, 48.
19. McKay, 142.
20. Wilson, 129.
21. Morrison, "Foreword," *Beloved*, xii.
22. Morrison, "Foreword," *Beloved*, xii.
23. Morrison, "A Conversation: Gloria Naylor," 208.
24. Morrison, "Charlie Rose: November 21, 2003."

25. Morrison, *Playing in the Dark*, 46, 44.
26. Morrison, "Foreword," *Jazz*, xi.
27. Morrison, "Charlie Rose: November 21, 2003."
28. Dreifus, 99.
29. Dreifus, 103.
30. See Houston, 232, for Morrison's comments on her choice of title.
31. Whitten, "Interview."
32. "Toni Morrison, Love," interview with Tavis Smiley.
33. Dowling, 54, Morrison's italics.

CHAPTER 2

1. For Morrison's comments on her use of the term "novel" and the functions of the European form, see Morrison, "Rootedness: The Ancestor as Foundation," 57–8.
2. Dubey, 151.
3. Rowe, 94.
4. See Dunn and Morris, *The Composite Novel*, and Kelley, "Gender and Genre."
5. Winfrey, "An Hour."
6. Ingram, 19. Ingram coined the term "short-story cycle."
7. Morrison, "Memory," 388.
8. Morrison, "Afterword," *The Bluest Eye*, 171.
9. Morrison, *The Bluest Eye*, 32.
10. Tate, 163.
11. Morrison, *Sula*, 174.
12. Tate, 163.
13. Morrison, "Foreword," *Song of Solomon*, x.
14. Morrison, *Tar Baby*, 57.
15. Morrison, "Foreword," *Jazz*, viii, ix.
16. Carabi, 94
17. Morrison, *Jazz*, 229.
18. "Book Club—Toni Morrison." See also Aubry, 357.
19. Ruas, 108.
20. Morrison, "Rootedness," 59, Morrison's italics.
21. Morrison, "Rootedness," 60.
22. Washington, 238, Morrison's italics.
23. Morrison, "The Site of Memory," 65, 69, 70.
24. In "The Site of Memory," Morrison notes that some slave narratives emulated the sentimental novel (69). Yellin writes in her introduction to Jacobs's *Incidents in the Life of a Slave Girl, Written by Herself* that

Jacobs deploys the language of the seduction novel: she "treats her sexual experiences obliquely, and when addressing the reader concerning her sexual behavior, pleads for forgiveness in the overwrought style of popular fiction" (xiv). Reddy sees structural affinities between Shadrack's story in *Sula* and the slave narrative. See her essay "The Tripled Plot and Center of *Sula*," 33.

25. Savoy, 167.
26. Hegerfeldt, "Magical Realism."
27. Darling, 248.
28. McKay, 152.

CHAPTER 3

1. Stepto, 22, Morrison's italics.
2. Tate, 158.
3. Morrison, "Fisherwoman," 140.

CHAPTER 4

1. McKay, 154.
2. Black Creation Annual, 8.
3. Koenen, 67.
4. Morrison, "Behind the Making of *The Black Book*," 36.
5. Brogan, 642.
6. Stepto, 14.

CHAPTER 5

1. Watkins, 46.
2. McKay, 144.
3. Black Creation Annual, 7.
4. Schappell, 84.

CHAPTER 6

1. Watkins, 47.
2. LeClair, 122.
3. Ruas, 102, Morrison's italics.
4. Ruas, 101–2.
5. Morrison, "Unspeakable Things Unspoken," 30.

CHAPTER 7

1. Washington, 235.
2. Darling, 247.
3. Morrison, "A Conversation: Gloria Naylor," 207, 208, Morrison's italics.
4. Morrison, "Audio Interview."
5. Morrison, "Rootedness," 58.
6. Caldwell, 243.
7. "Toni Morrison," Timehost interview.
8. Morrison, "Audio Interview."

CHAPTER 8

1. Morrison, "Rootedness," 59.
2. Davis, 233.
3. Micucci, 275.
4. Morrison, "Jazz Queen," 28.

CHAPTER 9

1. Morrison, *Paradise*, 3.
2. "Book Club—Toni Morrison," quoted in Aubry, 361.
3. Farnsworth, 156.
4. Morrison, "A Conversation: Gloria Naylor," 192–3.
5. Morrison, "An Hour."
6. "Book Club—Toni Morrison," quoted in Aubry, 357.

CHAPTER 10

1. Morrison, *Love*, 103.
2. Morrison, "Charlie Rose: November 21, 2003."
3. Houston, 228.

CHAPTER 11

1. Denard, "Blacks, Modernism," 191.
2. Silverblatt, 172.
3. Levander and Singley, 4.
4. Angelo, 260.
5. Morrison, "Dinner at Oprah's."
6. See Chapter 1, "Toni Morrison: A Writer's Life."
7. LeClair, 125.

8. Houston, 230.
9. LeClair, 126.
10. Koenen, 73.
11. Ruas, 112.
12. Davis, 229, Morrison's italics.
13. Morrison, "Charlie Rose: November 21, 2003."
14. Gates, *America Behind*, xiv.
15. Gates, *America Beyond*.
16. Gates, *America Behind*, 223.
17. "Toni Morrison," Timehost interview.
18. Israely, "*Vogue Italia*."
19. Johnston and Philippidou, "Black is Finally."
20. Morrison, "A Slow Walk," 3, 4, Morrison's italics.
21. Morrison, "On the Backs," 148.
22. Jaffrey, 150, 151.
23. Cooke, "'America.'"
24. See Chapter 14, "Toni Morrison and the Media" for further exploration of this perception.
25. Mcgeveran, "Toni Morrison's Letter."
26. "Toni Morrison: 'Election of Obama.'"

CHAPTER 12

1. Morrison, "On the Backs of Blacks," 145, 145–146.
2. Morrison, "Rediscovering Black History," 42.
3. Silverblatt, 173.
4. Morrison, "This Side of Paradise," interview with James Marcus.
5. Winfrey, "An Hour."
6. Winfrey, "An Hour."
7. Winfrey and Regan, *Journey*, 112.
8. Morrison, "The Site of Memory," 75.
9. Koolish, 428.
10. Wardi, 513.
11. Silverblatt, 174.
12. Winfrey and Regan, *Journey*, 138.
13. Conner, 215.
14. Joyner, "Film: Staying Stubbornly True."
15. Wardi, 522.
16. Tibberts, "Oprah's Belabored Beloved."
17. Silverblatt, 176.
18. Guthmann, "Ghost of Slavery."
19. Wardi, 514.

20. Weintraub, "'Beloved' Tests."
21. Weintraub, "'Beloved' Tests."
22. Gates, *Behind*, 274.
23. Conner, 204.
24. Whitten, "Interview."
25. Corliss, "Bewitching Beloved."
26. McGurk, "'Beloved' Masterpiece."

CHAPTER 13

1. McElrath, African-American History, About.com.
2. Morrison, "A Bench by the Road, *UU World* magazine."
3. VG: Voices from the Gaps: Women Artists and Writers of Color, an International Web site.
4. Weinstein, "Faulkner 101."
5. Morrison, "The Truest Eye."
6. Gray, "Paradise Found."
7. Scott, "In Search of the Best."
8. Morrison, "The Salon Interview."
9. "A Discussion about woman.life.song."
10. Neal, "Toni Morrison: Words of Love."
11. Capriccioso, "Toni Morrison's Challenge."

CHAPTER 14

1. Morrison, "The Nobel Lecture," 201.
2. Morrison, "Talk of the Town," 149.
3. Morrison, "Introduction: Friday on the Potomac," 8.
4. Morrison, "Introduction: Friday on the Potomac," xvi.
5. Morrison, "The Nobel Lecture," 203.
6. Morrison, "Introduction: Friday on the Potomac," 30.
7. Morrison, "The Official Story," xviii.
8. Harris, 9.
9. Morrison, "Charlie Rose: November 21, 2003."
10. Caldwell, 243, Morrison's italics.
11. Jaffrey, 140.
12. Morrison, "An Hour."
13. Jaffrey, 143.
14. LeClair, 125.
15. Morrison, "Toni Morrison, Love,"
16. Kakutani, "Books of the Times."
17. Morrison, "An Hour."

18. "The Toni Award," *The New Republic.*
19. Morrison, "Talk of the Town," 152.
20. "Toni Morrison," Timehost interview.
21. Gray, "Paradise Found."
22. Quoted in Rachel Cooke, "America is Going Backwards."
23. Morrison, "Charlie Rose: May 7, 1993."
24. Morrison, "*Sula*," http://www.oprah.com.
25. Farr, 1.
26. Max, 37.
27. Dreifus, 106.
28. "Book Club—Toni Morrison," quoted in Max, 39.
29. Young, 183.
30. Aubry, 356. Aubry gives an illuminating exploration of the dynamics at work between Morrison and the readers during the book club show devoted to *Paradise.*
31. For details of Franzen's comments, see Laura Miller, "Book Lovers' Quarrel."
32. Young, 187.
33. Morrison, "For a Heroic Writers' Movement," 160.
34. Young, 181.

CHAPTER 15

1. Morrison, "A Mother," interview with Lynn Neary.
2. Morrison, *A Mercy,* 76.
3. Morrison, "An Hour."
4. Gikandi, x.
5. Morrison, "On *The Radiance of the King*," 122.
6. Morrison, "A Conversation: Gloria Naylor," 213.
7. Gates, "Zora Neale Hurston," 200.
8. Simms, Washington, and Weller, "Paule Marshall."
9. Ibid.
10. Washington, 236.
11. Walker, "Saving the Life," 7.
12. See Melissa Walker's reading of both novels in *Down from the Mountaintop: Black Women's Novels in the Wake of the Civil Rights Movement.*
13. Morrison, "Preface to *Deep Sightings*," 87.
14. Naylor, *The Women of Brewster Place,* 60.
15. Jaffrey, 149.
16. Kincaid, *Annie John,* 147.
17. Douglass, *Narrative,* 51.
18. Morrison, "Toni Morrison on a Book," 109.

19. Quentin Miller, "Ellison, Ralph," 493.

20. Jaggi, "Solving the Riddle."

21. Morrison, "James Baldwin," 91.

22. Oates, "If Beale Street."

23. Dreifus, 101.

24. Watkins, 47.

25. Morrison, "Charlie Rose: November 21, 2003."

26. Welty, "Preface, *Collected Stories*," xi.

27. See the front cover of Louise Erdrich, *Love Medicine*.

28. "The Greatness of Gabriel García Márquez."

RESOURCES

Works by Toni Morrison

"Audio Interview with Toni Morrison." Interview with Don Swaim, CBS Radio, September 15, 1987. http://wiredforbooks.org/tonimorrison/ (accessed September 19, 2008).

"Behind the Making of *The Black Book*." In *What Moves at the Margin: Selected Nonfiction*, 34–8.

Beloved. (1987) Reprint, London: Vintage, 2005.

"A Bench by the Road." *UU World* magazine, January–February 1989. http://www.uuworld.org/ideas/articles/117810.shtml (accessed September 14, 2008).

"A Bench by the Road: *Beloved* by Toni Morrison." In Denard, *Toni Morrison*, 44–51.

Birth of a Nation'hood: Gaze, Script, and Spectacle in the O. J. Simpson Case, edited with Claudia Brodsky Lacour. London: Vintage, 1997.

The Bluest Eye. (1970) Reprint, London: Vintage, 1999.

"Charlie Rose: May 7, 1993 Interview." *Charlie Rose*. http://vodpod.com/watch/364928-charlie-rose-may-7-1993 (accessed September 19, 2008).

"Charlie Rose: November 21, 2003 Interview." *Charlie Rose*. http://www.charlierose.com/view/interview/1708 (accessed February 25, 2009).

"A Conversation: Gloria Naylor and Toni Morrison." In Taylor-Guthrie, *Conversations*, 188–217.

"Conversation: Toni Morrison." Interview with Elizabeth Farnsworth, *The NewsHour*, March 9, 1998. http://www.pbs.org/newshour/bb/entertainment/jan-june98/morrison_3-9.html (accessed September 26, 2008).

"The Dancing Mind." In *What Moves*, 187–90.

"Dinner at Oprah's: Toni Morrison 1996." *The Oprah Winfrey Show: 20th Anniversary Collection.* DVD. Harpo Productions, Inc., 2006.

"The Fisherwoman: Introduction to *A Kind of Rapture: Photographs.*" In *What Moves,* 138–42.

"For a Heroic Writers' Movement." In *What Moves,* 156–63.

"An Hour with Nobel Prize-Winning Author Toni Morrison." Interview with Charlie Rose, March 16, 1998. http://www.charlierose.com/view/interview/5041 (accessed June 24, 2009).

"Introduction: Friday on the Potomac." In *Race-ing,* vii–xxx.

"James Baldwin: His Voice Remembered; Life in His Language." In *What Moves,* 90–4.

Jazz. (1992) Reprint, London: Vintage, 2005.

"Jazz Queen." Interview with Christopher Bigsby. *Independent,* April 26, 1992: 28–9.

Love. (2003) Reprint, London: Vintage, 2004.

"Memory, Creation, and Writing." *Thought* 59 (1984): 385–9.

A Mercy. London: Chatto and Windus, 2008.

"A Mother, A Stranger, A Mercy." Interview with Lynn Neary, NPR. October 27, 2008. http://www.npr.org/templates/story/story.php?storyID=95961382 (accessed May 4, 2009).

"The Nobel Lecture in Literature." In *What Moves,* 198–207.

"The Official Story: Dead Man Golfing: Introduction by Toni Morrison." In Morrison and Lacour, *Birth of a Nation'hood,* vii–xxviii.

"On the Backs of Blacks." In *What Moves,* 145–8.

"On *The Radiance of the King.*" In *What Moves,* 118–34.

Paradise. (1998) Reprint, London: Vintage, 1999.

Playing in the Dark: Whiteness and the Literary Imagination. (1992) Reprint, London: Picador-Macmillan, 1993.

"Preface to *Deep Sightings and Rescue Missions* by Toni Cade Bambara." In *What Moves,* 86–9.

Race-ing Justice, En-Gendering Power: Essays on Anita Hill, Clarence Thomas, and the Construction of Social Reality (editor). London: Chatto, 1993.

"Rediscovering Black History." In *What Moves,* 39–55.

"Rootedness: The Ancestor as Foundation." In *What Moves,* 56–64.

"The Salon Interview." Interview with Zia Jaffrey, Salon.com, February 2, 1998. http://www.salon.com/books/int/1998/02/02/cov_si_02int/index.html (accessed September 20, 2008).

"The Site of Memory." In *What Moves,* 65–80.

"A Slow Walk of Trees (as Grandmother Would Say), Hopeless (as Grandfather Would Say)." In *What Moves,* 3–14.

Song of Solomon. (1977) Reprint, London: Vintage, 2005.

Sula. (1973) Reprint, London: Vintage, 2005.

"The Talk of the Town." In *What Moves*, 149–53.

Tar Baby. (1981) Reprint, London: Vintage, 1997.

"This Side of Paradise." Interview with James Marcus, September 18, 2008. http://www.amazon.com/gp/feature.html?ie=UTF8&docId=7651 (accessed May 4, 2009).

"Toni Morrison, Love." Interview with Tavis Smiley, NPR, October 3, 2003. http://www.npr.org/templates/story/story.php?storyId=1484643 (accessed May 4, 2009).

"Toni Morrison on a Book She Loves: Gayl Jones's *Corregidora*." In *What Moves*, 108–10.

"The Truest Eye." Interview with Pam Houston, *O, The Oprah Magazine*, November 2003. http://www.oprah.com/article/omagazine/omag_200311_toni/1 (accessed. September 20, 2008).

"Unspeakable Things Unspoken." *Michigan Quarterly Review* XXVIII (Winter 1989): 1–35.

What Moves at the Margin: Selected Nonfiction. Edited by Carolyn C. Denard. Jackson: University Press of Mississippi, 2008.

OTHER RESOURCES

Achebe, Chinua. *Things Fall Apart*. African Writers Series. (1958) Reprint, Oxford: Heinemann Education, 2000.

"African American History." University of Washington Library. http://www.lib.washington.edu/subject/History/tm/black/html (accessed September 20, 2008).

Angelo, Bonnie. "The Pain of Being Black: An Interview with Toni Morrison." In Taylor-Guthrie, *Conversations*, 255–61.

Angelou, Maya. *I Know Why the Caged Bird Sings*. (1970) Reprint, London: Virago, 1984.

"Anniina's Toni Morrison Page." http://www.luminarium.org/contemporary/tonimorrison/toni.htm (accessed September 19, 2008).

Aubry, Timothy. "Beware the Furrow of the Middlebrow: Searching for *Paradise* on *The Oprah Winfrey Show*." *Modern Fiction Studies* 52.2 (Summer 2006): 350–73.

"Author Spotlight: Toni Morrison." Random House. http://www.randomhouse.com/author/results.pperl?authorid=21332 (accessed September 19, 2008).

Bakerman, Jane. "The Seams Can't Show: An Interview with Toni Morrison." In Taylor-Guthrie, *Conversations*, 30–42.

Baldwin, James. *If Beale Street Could Talk*. (1974) Reprint, London: Penguin, 1994.

Black Creation Annual. "Conversations with Alice Childress and Toni Morrison." In Taylor-Guthrie, *Conversations*, 3–10.

"*The Bluest Eye.*" Oprah's Book Club. http://www.oprah.com/article/oprahs bookclub/pastselections/obc_20000427_aboutauthor (accessed September 20, 2008).

"Book Club—Toni Morrison." *The Oprah Winfrey Show.* Harpo Productions, Inc., March 6, 1998.

Brogan, Hugh. *The Penguin History of the USA.* (1985) Reprint, London: Penguin, 1999.

Brown, Cecil. "Interview with Toni Morrison." In Denard, *Toni Morrison,* 107–125.

Caldwell, Gail. "Author Toni Morrison Discusses Her Latest Novel *Beloved.*" In Taylor-Guthrie, *Conversations,* 239–45.

Capriccioso, Rob. "Toni Morrison's Challenge." Connect for Kids, July 25, 2003. http://www.connectforkids.org/node/487 (accessed February 15, 2009).

Carabi, Angels. "Nobel Laureate Toni Morrison Speaks about Her Novel *Jazz.*" In Denard, *Toni Morrison,* 91–7.

Conner, Marc C. "The Specter of History: Filming Memory in *Beloved.*" In *Twentieth-Century American Fiction on Screen,* edited by R. Barton Palmer. Cambridge: Cambridge University Press, 2007, 202–16.

Cooke, Rachel. "'America is Going Backwards.'" *The Observer,* September 19, 2004. http://www.guardian.co.uk/books/2004/sep/19/fiction.tonimorrison (accessed December 19, 2008).

Corliss, Richard. "Bewitching Beloved." *Time,* October 5, 1998. http://www.time.com/time/magazine/article/0,9171,989239,00.html (accessed September 20, 2008).

Darling, Marsha. "In the Realm of Responsibility: A Conversation with Toni Morrison." In Taylor-Guthrie, *Conversations,* 246–54.

Davis, Christina. "An Interview with Toni Morrison." In Taylor-Guthrie, *Conversations,* 223–33.

Demme, Jonathan, director. *Beloved.* (1998) DVD. Buena Vista, 2001.

Denard, Carolyn C. "Blacks, Modernism, and the American South: An Interview with Toni Morrison." In Denard, *Toni Morrison,* 178–95. http://findarticles.com/p/articles/mi_qa3822/is_199810/ai_n8818833/ (accessed May 4, 2009).

———, ed. *Toni Morrison: Conversations.* Literary Conversations Series. Jackson: University Press of Mississippi, 2008.

"A Discussion about woman.life.song with Jessye Norman, Toni Morrison, Clarissa Pinkola Estés, and Judith Weir." *Charlie Rose,* March 20, 2000. http://www.charlierose.com/view/interview/3795 (accessed September 18, 2008).

Douglass, Frederick. *Narrative of the Life of Frederick Douglass, an American Slave, Written by Himself.* (1845) Reprint, London: Penguin, 1982.

Dowling, Colette. "The Song of Toni Morrison." In Taylor-Guthrie, *Conversations*, 48–59.

Dreifus, Claudia. "Chloe Wofford Talks about Toni Morrison." In Denard, *Toni Morrison*, 98–107.

Dubey, Madhu. "African-American Fiction and the Politics of Postmodernism." *Novel: A Forum on Fiction* 35 (2002): 151–68.

Dunn, Maggie and Ann Morris. *The Composite Novel: The Short Story Cycle in Transition*. Twayne's Studies in Literary Themes and Genres 6. New York: Twayne/Macmillan, 1995.

Duvall, John N. "Descent in the 'House of Chloe': Race, Rape, and Identity in Toni Morrison's *Tar Baby*." *Contemporary Literature* 38.2 (Summer 1997): 325–49.

Ellison, Ralph. *Invisible Man*. (1952) Reprint, London: Penguin, 1965.

Erdrich, Louise. *Love Medicine*. London: HarperCollins-Flamingo, 1994.

Farnsworth, Elizabeth. "Conversation: Toni Morrison." In Denard, *Toni Morrison*, 155–8.

Farr, Cecilia Konchar. *Reading Oprah: How Oprah's Book Club Changed the Way America Reads*. Albany: State University of New York Press, 2005.

Faulkner, William. *Go Down, Moses*. (1942) Reprint, London: Vintage, 1991.

Gates, Henry Louis, Jr. *America Behind the Color Line: Dialogues with African Americans*. New York: Warner, 2004.

———. *America Beyond the Color Line with Henry Louis Gates, Jr.* (2003) DVD. Artwork PBS, 2005.

———. *Loose Canons: Notes on the Culture Wars*. New York: Oxford University Press, 1992.

———. *The Signifying Monkey: A Theory of Afro-American Literary Criticism*. New York: Oxford University Press, 1980.

———. "Zora Neale Hurston and the Speakerly Text." In Gates, *The Signifying Monkey*, 170–216.

Gikandi, Simon. "Chinua Achebe and the Invention of African Literature." In Achebe, *Things Fall Apart*, ix–xvii.

Gray, Paul. "Paradise Found." *Time*, January 19, 1998. http://www.time.com/time/magazine/article/0,9171,987690,00.html (accessed September 18, 2008).

"The Greatness of Gabriel García Márquez." Books Blog, March 8, 2007. http://www.guardian.co.uk/books/booksblog/2007/mar/08/thegreatnessofgabrielgarci (accessed May 4, 2009).

Guthmann, Edward. "Ghost of Slavery." *San Francisco Chronicle*, October 16, 1998. http://www.sfgate.com/cgi-bin/article.cgi?f=/c/a/1998/10/16/DD16762.DTL (accessed September 19, 2008).

Harris, Jessica. "'I Will Always Be a Writer.'" In Denard, *Toni Morrison*, 3–9.

Hegerfeldt, Anne. "Magical Realism." *The Literary Encyclopedia*, 2009. http://www.litencyc.com/php/stopics.php?rec=true&UID=682   (accessed May 4, 2009).

Hostetler, Ann. "Interview with Toni Morrison: 'The Art of Teaching.'" In Denard, *Toni Morrison*, 196–205.

Houston, Pam. "Pam Houston Talks with Toni Morrison." In Denard, *Toni Morrison,* 228–59.

Hurston, Zora Neale. *Their Eyes Were Watching God*. (1937) Reprint, London: Virago, 1986.

Ingram, Forrest L. *Representative Short Story Cycles of the Twentieth Century: Studies in a Literary Genre*. The Hague, Netherlands: Mouton, 1971.

Israely, Jeff. "*Vogue Italia* Is a Hit in Black." *Time*, July 30, 2008. http://www.time.com/time/arts/article/0,8599,1828063,00.html   (accessed May 4, 2009).

Jacobs, Harriet Brent. *Incidents in the Life of a Slave Girl, Written by Herself.* (1861) Reprint, New York: Dover, 2001.

Jaffrey, Zia. "Toni Morrison." In Denard, *Toni Morrison*, 139–54.

Jaggi, Maya. "Solving the Riddle." *The Guardian,* November 15, 2003. http://www.guardian.co.uk/books/2003/nov/15/fiction.tonimorrison.   (accessed September 17, 2008).

Johnston, Ian and Photini Philippidou. "Black is Finally in Fashion at Vogue." *Independent,* April 27, 2008. http://www.independent.co.uk/life-style/fashion/news/black-is-finally-in-fashion-at-vogue-816213.html   (accessed September 17, 2008).

Jones, Gayl. *Corregidora*. (1975) Reprint, London: Serpent's, 2000.

Joyner, Will. "Film: Staying Stubbornly True to a Writer's Vision." *New York Times,* October 18, 1998. http://www.nytimes.com/1998/10/18/movies/film-staying-stubbornly-true-to-a-writer-s-vision.html?pagewanted=all (accessed May 4, 2009).

Kakutani, Michiko. "Books of the Times: 'Paradise': Worthy Women, Unredeemable Men." *New York Times*, January 6, 1998. http://www.nytimes.com/books/98/01/04/daily/morrison-book-review-art.html?scp=1&sq=Worthy%20Women,%20Unredeemable%20Men."%20&st=cse   (accessed May 4, 2009).

Kelley, Margot Anne. "Gender and Genre: The Case of the Novel-in-Stories." In *American Women Short Story Writers: A Collection of Critical Essays,* edited by Julie Brown. Wellesley Studies in Critical Theory, Literary History, and Culture. New York: Garland, 1995, 295–310.

Kincaid, Jamaica. *Annie John*. (1985) Reprint, London: Vintage, 1997.

Kingston, Maxine Hong. *The Woman Warrior: Memoirs of a Girlhood Among Ghosts*. (1976) Reprint, New York: Vintage-Random, 1977.

Koenen, Anne. "The One Out of Sequence." In Taylor-Guthrie, *Conversations*, 67–83.

Koolish, Lynda. "Fictive Strategies and Cinematic Representations in Toni Morrison's *Beloved*: Postcolonial Theory/Postcolonial Text." *African American Review* 29.3 (Autumn 1995): 421–38.

Langer, Adam. "Star Power." In Denard, *Toni Morrison*, 206–13.

Laye, Camara. *The Radiance of the King*. New York: NYRB Classics, 2001.

LeClair, Thomas. "The Language Must Not Sweat: A Conversation with Toni Morrison." In Taylor-Guthrie, *Conversations*, 119–128.

Lee, Felicia. "Bench of Memory at Slavery's Gateway." *New York Times*, July 28, 2008.   http://www.nytimes.com/2008/07/28/arts/design/28benc.html?hp (accessed September 18, 2008).

Levander, Caroline and Carol J. Singley, eds. *The American Child: A Cultural Studies Reader*. New Brunswick, NJ: Rutgers, 2003.

Márquez, Gabriel García. *One Hundred Years of Solitude*. (1967) Reprint, New York: Harper-Perennial, 1998.

Marshall, Paule. *Brown Girl, Brown Stones*. Contemporary Classics by Women. (1959) Reprint, New York: The Feminist Press at CUNY, 2006.

Maslin, Janet. "Beloved: No Peace from a Brutal Legacy." *New York Times*, October 16, 1998. http://movies.nytimes.com/movie/review?res=9405E4 D8133AF935A25753C1A96E958260&scp=1&sq=Beloved%20movie% 20review&st=cse (accessed September 19, 2008).

Max, D. T. "The Oprah Effect." *New York Times Magazine*, December 26, 1999, 36–41.

McCluskey, Audrey T. "A Conversation with Toni Morrison." In Denard, *Toni Morrison*, 38–43.

McElrath, Jessica. "African-American History." About.com. http://afroam history.about.com/mbiopage.htm (accessed September 15, 2008).

Mcgeveran, Tom. "Toni Morrison's Letter to Barack Obama." *New York Observer*, January 28, 2008. http://www.observer.com/2008/toni-morrisons-letter-barack-obama (accessed December 19, 2008).

McGurk, Margaret A. "'Beloved' Masterpiece." *Cincinnati Enquirer*, October 16, 1998. http://www.cincinnati.com/freetime/movies/mcgurk/beloved. html (accessed May 4, 2009).

McKay, Nellie. "An Interview with Toni Morrison." Taylor-Guthrie, *Conversations*, 138–155.

Micucci, Dana. "An Inspired Life: Toni Morrison Writes and a Generation Listens." In Taylor-Guthrie, *Conversations*, 275–9.

Miller, Laura. "Book Lovers' Quarrel." Salon.com, October 26, 2001. http:// archive.salon.com/books/feature/2001/10/26/franzen_winfrey (accessed September 18, 2008).

Miller, Quentin. "Ellison, Ralph." In *The Greenwood Encyclopedia of African American Literature,* Vol. 2, edited by Hans Ostrom and J. David Macey Jr. Westport, CT: Greenwood, 2005, 492–7.

Naylor, Gloria. *Bailey's Café.* New York: Harcourt, 1992.

———. *The Men of Brewster Place.* New York: Hyperion, 1998.

———. *The Women of Brewster Place.* Penguin Contemporary American Fiction. (1982) Reprint, New York: Penguin, 1983.

Neal, Rome. "Toni Morrison: Words of Love." CBS News, April 2, 2004. http://www.cbsnews.com/stories/2004/04/02/Sunday/main610053.shtml (accessed February 21, 2009).

Neustadt, Kathy. "The Visits of the Writers Toni Morrison and Eudora Welty." In Taylor-Guthrie, *Conversations,* 84–92.

Oates, Joyce Carol. "If Beale Street Could Talk." Review, *New York Times,* May 19, 1974. http://www.nytimes.com/books/98/03/29/baldwin-beale.html (accessed June 25, 2009).

"*Paradise* by Toni Morrison." Oprah's Book Club. http://www.oprah.com/article/oprahsbookclub/pastselections/obc_pb_19980116_about (accessed September 20, 2008).

Parker, Betty Jean. "Complexity: Toni Morrison's Women." In Taylor-Guthrie, *Conversations,* 60–66.

Reddy, Maureen T. "The Tripled Plot and Center of *Sula*." *Black Literature Forum* 221.1 (Spring 1988): 29–45.

Rowe, John Carlos. "The African-American Voice in Faulkner's *Go Down, Moses*." *Modern Short Story Sequences: Composite Fictions and Fictive Communities,* edited by J. Gerald Kennedy. Cambridge: Cambridge University Press, 1995, 76–97.

Ruas, Charles. "Toni Morrison." In Taylor-Guthrie, *Conversations,* 93–118.

Sachs, Andrea. "10 Questions for Toni Morrison." *Time,* May 7, 2008. http://www.time.com/arts/article/0,8599,1738303,00.html.

Savoy, Eric. "The Rise of the American Gothic." In *The Cambridge Companion to Gothic Fiction,* edited by Jerrold E. Hogle. Cambridge: Cambridge University Press, 2002, 167–89.

Schappell, Elisa. "Toni Morrison: The Art of Fiction." In Denard, *Toni Morrison,* 62–90.

Scott, A. O. "In Search of the Best." *New York Times Book Review,* May 21, 2006. http://www.nytimes.com/2006/05/21/books/review/scott-essay.html?scp=1&sq=%93In%20Search%20of%20the%20Best.%94%20&st=cse (accessed May 4, 2009).

Silverblatt, Michael. "'Things We Find in Language:' A Conversation with Toni Morrison." In Denard, *Toni Morrison,* 171–77.

Simms, Alicia, Sharlene Washington, and Talmage Weller. "Paule Marshall b. 1929." May 23, 2001. VG: Voices from the Gaps: Women

Artists and Writers of Color, an International Website. http://voices. cla.umn.edu/vg/Bios/entries/marshall_paule.html (accessed September 15, 2008).

Smiley, Jane. "Ghosts of a Brutal Past." *The Guardian*, July 7, 2006. http:// www.guardian.co.uk/books/2006/jul/08/fiction.tonimorrison (accessed September 12, 2008).

"*Song of Solomon*." Oprah's Book Club. http://www.oprah.com/article/ oprahsbookclub/pastselections/obc_pb_19961018_about (accessed May 4, 2009).

Stepto, Robert. "Intimate Things in Place: A Conversation with Toni Morrison." In Taylor-Guthrie, *Conversations*, 10–39.

"*Sula*." Oprah's Book Club. http://www.oprah.com/article/oprahsbookclub/ pastselections/obc_20020405_about (accessed September 20, 2008).

"*Sula* Discussion." Oprah's Book Club. http://www.oprah.com/article/oprahs bookclub/pastselections/obc_20020502_discussion (accessed September 20, 2008).

"*Sula*" Discussion Group Members." Oprah's Book Club. http://www.oprah. com/article/oprahsbookclub/pastselections/obc_20020502_letters (accessed September 19, 2008).

Tate, Claudia. "Toni Morrison." In Taylor-Guthrie, *Conversations*, 156–170.

Taylor-Guthrie, Danielle, ed. *Conversations with Toni Morrison*. Literary Conversations Series. Jackson: University Press of Mississippi, 1994.

Tibberts, John C. "Oprah's Belabored Beloved." *Literature Film Quarterly* (1999): 74–6.

"The Toni Award." *The New Republic*, June 19, 1989, 9–10.

"Toni Morrison." A Timehost Interview. *Time*, January 21, 1998. http://www. time.com/time/community/transcripts/chattr012198.html (accessed September 20, 2008).

"Toni Morrison b. 1931." VG: Voices from the Gaps: Women Artists and Writers of Color, an International Website. http://voices.cla.umn.edu/vg/ Bios/entries/morrison_toni.html (accessed September 19, 2008).

"Toni Morrison: 'Election of Obama Was Courageous.'" November 19, 2008. http://fora.tv/2008/11/19/An_Evening_with_Toni_Morrison#chapter_01 (accessed May 4, 2009).

Walker, Alice. *The Color Purple*. (1982), Reprint, London: Women's Press, 1983.

———. *Meridian*. (1976) Reprint, London: Women's Press, 2001.

———. "Saving the Life that Is Your Own: The Importance of Models in the Artist's Life." In *In Search of Our Mothers' Gardens: Womanist Prose*. London: Women's Press, 1984, 3–14.

Walker, Melissa. *Down from the Mountaintop: Black Women's Novels in the Wake of the Civil Rights Movement, 1966–1989*. New Haven, CT: Yale University Press, 1991.

Wardi, Anissa Janine. "Freak Shows, Spectacles, and Carnivals: Reading Jonathan Demme's Beloved." *African-American Review* (Winter 2005): 513–26.

Washington, Elsie B. "Talk with Toni Morrison." In Taylor-Guthrie, *Conversations*, 234–8.

Watkins, Mel. "Talk with Toni Morrison." In Taylor-Guthrie, *Conversations*, 43–7.

Weinstein, Philip. "Faulkner 101: Toni Morrison and William Faulkner." Oprah's Book Club. http://www.oprah.com/article/oprahsbookclub/past selections/books_morrison/1 (accessed September 10, 2008).

Weintraub, Bernard. "'Beloved' Tests Racial Themes at Box Office; Will This Winfrey Film Appeal to White Audiences?" *New York Times*, October 13, 1998. http://www.nytimes.com/1998/10/13/movies/beloved-tests-racial-themes-box-office-will-this-winfrey-film-appeal-white.html?sec=&spon=&&scp=1&sq=Beloved'%20Tests%20Racial%20Themes%20&st=cse (accessed May 4, 2009).

Welty, Eudora. *The Collected Stories of Eudora Welty*. London: Penguin, 1983.

———. *The Eye of the Story: Selected Essays and Reviews*. (1979) Reprint, London: Virago, 1987.

Whitten, Robin F. "Interview: Talking with Toni Morrison." Audiofile, December 1998/January 1999. http://www.audiofilemagazine.com/features/AO419.html (accessed May 4, 2009).

Williams, Sherley Anne. *Dessa Rose: A Novel*. (1986) Reprint, New York: Harper Perennial, 1999.

Wilson, Judith. "A Conversation with Toni Morrison." In Taylor-Guthrie, *Conversations*, 129–37.

Winfrey, Oprah. "An Hour with Oprah Winfrey about the Film 'Beloved.'" Charlie Rose, October 29, 1998. http://www.charlierose.com/shows/1998/10/29/1/an-hour-with-oprah-winfrey-about-the-film-beloved (accessed September 20, 2008).

Winfrey, Oprah and Ken Regan. *Journey to Beloved*. New York: Hyperion, 1998.

Yellin, Jean Fagan. "Introduction." In *Incidents in the Life of a Slave Girl, Written by Herself*, by Harriet Brent Jacobs. Cambridge, MA: Harvard University Press, 1987, xiii–xxxiv.

Young, John. "Toni Morrison, Oprah Winfrey, and Postmodern Popular Audiences." *African American Review* 35.2 (Summer 2001): 181–204.

INDEX